Bernie Hammond, 1981

Someone Has to Pop the Corn

Author's Note

This is a true story. However, some of the names, places, and circumstances have been disguised to protect the privacy of those involved. Some of the key characters are composites of people we have known as we worked to make "Always on Thursday" our motto.

Any reference to "our town" could mean either of the two finest communities in Indiana. Both towns were so long a part of our lives that they will remain forever as one.

All Bible verses are from the Revised Standard Version of the Bible, copyrighted 1946 and 1952 by the Division of Christian Education of the National Council of the Churches of Christ in the United States of America.

Ann Kindig Sheetz

Someone Has to Pop the Corn

ANN KINDIG SHEETZ

CHRISTIAN HERALD BOOKS
Chappaqua, New York 10514

This book is dedicated to Loren, Todd, and Doug, to 2100 loyal subscribers, and to the Editor-in-Chief who answered all our prayers as we struggled to make "Always on Thursday" our motto

Copyright © 1981 by Ann Kindig Sheetz

Library of Congress Cataloging in Publication Data
Sheetz, Ann Kindig.
   Someone has to pop the corn.

   1. Journalists—United States—Biography. 2. Sheets family. 3. Christian life—1960-
I. Title.
PN4871.S5   070'.92'4 [B]   81-65728
ISBN 0-915684-96-9   AACR2

MEMBER OF
EVANGELICAL CHRISTIAN
PUBLISHERS ASSOCIATION

Christian Herald, independent, evangelical and interdenominational is dedicated to publishing wholesome, inspirational and religious books for Christian families.

First Edition
CHRISTIAN HERALD BOOKS, 40 Overlook Drive, Chappaqua, New York 10514
Printed in the United States of America

Contents

1

A Camel Caravan Goes Weekly

Snug in parkas, boots, and gloves and armed with notebooks and cameras, we set off on the day's outing. Our destination was undetermined, our goal a pictorial essay of the aftermath of a blizzard.

Todd scrunched in the corner of the back seat clutching his camera. Eight going on twenty-one, he envisioned himself as Todd the Photographer, *the* photographer who would get a perfect picture of a deer silhouetted against snow-covered pines. He rode in silence, glaring out the window in search of the elusive animals. Occasionally, he shouted, "Mom, look on the other side of the road! This is my side. If you see a deer, yell."

Doug, not quite two, was an even less stoic traveler. As he became too warm his mittens flew through the air like blind bats and his zipper yielded to little fingers, giving his coat freedom to flap wildly as he jumped with excitement. The powerful springs that seemed to be built into his legs uncoiled constantly, orbiting him across the back of the seat and onto my neck, the top of my head or, if his aim was good enough, smack in the middle of my lap.

The expedition returned hours later with pictures of pines heavy with snow and a few intrepid ice fishermen. Appetites, however, were unlimited. Now was the time for exotic food and stimulating conversation such as I'd dreamed of when I'd envisioned myself as a globe-trotting journalist who took to the desert by camel caravan. But it was the oven of my electric range, not a remote charcoal or camel dung fire, that produced beef heart stuffed with dressing and corn muffins that joined vegetables, fruit, and milk on the menu. Conversation tended to range from, "Doug, get your feet off the table," to "Todd, quit leaning on your elbow," but the aura of excitement prevailed, and spilled milk flowed freely.

Later, as the debris in the kitchen gave way to order and Doug had been tucked in for a nap while Todd hung up his camera in favor of a third grade scientific journal, we took time to settle back for second cups of tea and coffee and reflect on how it was that our dreams had brought us to this point.

"I never really took you seriously when you said you wanted to own the *News*," Loren was saying. "I thought if I agreed, you'd forget it." His words were partially serious but mostly in jest. I'd heard them many times and I tuned him out as my mind wandered back to the day answered prayer had become a reality, the day a camel caravan had gone weekly.

I remembered how my heart hammered with joy as I watched Loren mount the operator's platform of our press.

Our press! The words were music to my ears, their sound blending in perfect harmony with the reluctant but powerful hum of the old press as its huge bed moved back and forth and sheets of newsprint were caught up by dozens of suction fingers and carried across its ancient cylinder.

"Thank You! Thank You! Thank You!" I whispered. The words seemed inadequate in relation to the joy I felt, but I knew the merciful God who had helped my wildest dreams come true would hear them as surely as if I shouted them from the top of the press or by swinging from the Linotype. In the ball game of life, He had put me in charge of the popcorn concession, an observer content to add the fluff to life, one easily moved to tears or laughter but not given to frenetic hops, leaps, and squeals of joy. For me to have become a cheerleader now would have been as inappropriate as whistling during a funeral or laughing at war.

Besides, I stood in awe of the entire operation that had suddenly become ours: lock, stock, press, and monthly payments. The smell of the ink, the clatter of the Linotype, the faintly acrid aroma of its gas-fired pot, and the slow but deliberate motion of the press created a heady atmosphere that seemed far superior to any of the glories of a perfect September day outside.

"Thank You, thank You," I whispered again, close to tears of joy as Loren turned and gave me a wink and a smile that nine years of marriage had taught me meant, "Here we go. This is it."

I turned again to my typewriter, surrounded by scrawled notes taken at a meeting the night before, and attempted to make sense out of them, but my adrenalin was pumping so furiously it was hard to concentrate. "This is it! We're doing it!" my mind shouted, but my fingers refused to take orders from a brain reeling with the realization of what had happened: We actually owned our own weekly newspaper—and not just any newspaper but the *News,* our hometown paper!

We've come a long way since high school, I reflected as I permitted my concentration to wander, watching in fascination as the printed pages descended into the stacker unit at the end of the press.

Loren was a farm boy who liked things mechanical. I was a farm girl who yearned to write. Together we had worked on the school paper, I as editor and he as mimeograph operator. And when my editing chores were ended (and with them the time-consuming job of typing the news in column form with "½" marks where the retyping should be squeezed or slash marks where added space was needed), he sometimes deemed me coordinated enough to slip sheet. As we worked, we talked of our goals. He wanted to work with his hands, to eventually own a business of his own. I wanted to be a writer.

"Printer's ink gets into your veins," I said.

"I don't know about that," he replied ruefully as he rubbed his shirt, "but it sure gets on your clothes."

Despite his down-to-earth approach to things poetic, we began to date, and after graduation he turned to a job that was mechanical while I went to work in a bank to earn money for college so I could learn to write. The *News* office and the bank shared the same building, but the closest I came to the pressroom was choking at the pungent odor of mats being cast that drifted into the basement. Across the wall people were writing, were watching their words being set into type. The thought was tantalizing, but simple economics told me I was better off at the bank earning money for college.

I didn't plan to fall in love during my freshman year, but the friendship that began at the mimeograph machine soon ripened into something deeper, and I cheerfully let marriage cut my college career short. "I can write just fine right here," I said as I installed a typewriter in an extra bedroom and began a rejection slip collection that reflected the best of the literary '50s.

My house was spotless, my writing materials orderly, the rejections depressing, although sometimes hopeful. But I soon learned the hard way that writing is a solitary profession, one in which the writer's tender ego is often bruised not only by editors but also by friends who don't understand that an extra cup of coffee can cut into writing time or by family and friends who find no favor with one who can put feelings into words but cannot always be moved to sweeping or dusting. There's something demoralizing about hearing a well-meaning acquaintance say, "She may be a writer, but she sure can't keep house." And besides, no one else we knew was a writer or even trying to be one. But I kept right on trying—but not until I had every window clean, every speck of dust eliminated. In my antiseptic world I came to miss people so much that my characters became flat, one-dimensional, uninteresting phantoms who moved like automatons in their own sterilized and disinfected worlds.

It wasn't surprising that I was again working at the bank when the draft interrupted our lives and sent Loren to Germany as a mechanic. I went, too, my typewriter, dictionary, and thesaurus in hand, but, instead of a best seller, I produced hundreds of letters—and a baby. And, next to the birth of Todd, we discovered that the biggest event in our lives was the arrival of the *News*. Hungry for news of family and friends no one thought to include in their letters, we cherished every word in the papers that arrived four at a time and at least a month late.

A new dream began to take shape.

"I'd like to own that paper someday," I said.

"Uh huh," Loren agreed absently as he read.

"Why not? You're mechanical. You could print it. I could write it."

"Maybe."

But the next time I mentioned it, he murmured, "Might not be a bad idea. You write it and I'll print it."

I was hearing the affirmation of a principle I would discuss with friends for years: The second time you hear something, it's not as offensive as it was the first time. By the time you've heard it a hundred times, it's not tasteless any longer. Using this principle helped my friend Agatha get used to her husband's hog operation. She said she couldn't stand the aroma of the pens; he said they smelled like money. Within a few months, she was agreeing with him, not even noticing the unsavory Eau de Pig that filtered over their entire farm. Another friend repeated, "Fat's where it's at," so often she didn't mind a few extra bulges. Unfortunately, the same tendency has often made us accept something we really dislike: legislation, advertising—the list is endless and often tasteless. But the results are the same.

Now I was seeing the same results with Loren, but while he was giving assent, we were five thousand miles from home with a military obligation yet to complete. Owning the *News* was something we seldom talked about seriously, but it was a dream I cherished even if I didn't give much thought to the possibility that it might come true.

Our first stop on returning to the States was at the *News* office, by then moved to a shiny new building on a quiet, tree-lined street. The owner was glad to see us, but he didn't say anything about selling the paper. Since we figured you didn't just go up to an editor and say, "Hey, do you want to sell your paper?" we turned to the priorities of reestablishing our home after a two-year interruption and to the obligations of parenthood, a role we found we enjoyed after being childless nearly five years.

Determined to be an immaculate housekeeper and devoted mother who wrote, I moved my typewriter from the dining room to a bedroom and to the den while I drafted a book as flat as a homemade cracker. I couldn't understand why I wanted to write when obviously I was a people person, but the desire was there. Discipline was lacking, but I had yet to learn it is a word that applies not only to children but to anyone, in any situation. I was soon back at work in a bank, and I had begun to think debits and credits had forever replaced printer's ink in my veins when I went to a meeting that broke down into an old-fashioned gabfest like the ones we'd had in college or at meetings of economy wives.

Everyone, it seemed, wanted to do something she was not doing. Sandra Mulligan wanted more degrees. Peggy Hall wanted a baby so badly she was considering artificial insemination. Polly Wright wanted a new sports car. Nancy Carter wanted her husband, Paul, to come to like their plumbing business as well as her late father had. Ruby Pearl wanted more customers for the department store she operated with her husband. I wanted to own the *News*.

Martina Singleton, who wanted nothing more than to find a new occupation for her husband, overheard my remark and told her husband, Russ. Russ fully understood the desire to do something different, having only recently hung up his traveling salesman's hat in favor of a more stable existence as a real estate agent, and he did what we had failed to do four years earlier. He marched into the newspaper office and demanded, "You want to sell?"

"I sure do," the owner replied.

Loren was again working as a mechanic, and when he slid out from under a car, he found Russ looking down at him, his freckled face creased into a broad grin. "You want to buy the *News*?"

It was an abrupt question, one he had not expected, but it repeated the litany he had heard me express ever since I realized the camel caravan and submarine excursions weren't going to be. "Sure, why not?" he said.

2

Always on Thursday

A small town doesn't really need a newspaper to spread the news. Word of mouth carries it faster than any weekly publication can hope to. The slogan hanging in half the businesses in town sums it up: "There's not much to see or do in a small town,. but what you hear makes up for the rest." Within an hour, Russ had told Hattie Hooper who told Sophie Palmer who told Silas Monroe who told Ruby Pearl who told everyone in the drugstore. The news spread from there to the restaurant and on down the street to the stores and shops that Loren and Ann Sheetz were going to purchase the *News*.

"They had any experience?"

"None."

"She's working in a bank and he's a good mechanic. Why do they want it?"

"She's going to write it and he's going to print it."

"Sounds crazy to me. Who'd want to own a newspaper in a town as small as this?"

We would, that's who. True, the town had only a thousand residents, but they had a thousand friendly faces. It was a community that stood by its members in sickness and in health—and in death. Benefit fish fries and bake sales had financed many a long hospitalization and had helped pay funeral expenses. It was a town in which the bank president mowed his own lawn wearing baggy shorts and red sneakers and where everyone was on a first name basis. It was a town that had been so much a part of both our families for more than a century that a trip to the cemetery was the same as a genealogical search. It was a town Loren and I had lived in all our lives. We had attended school in the same building that educated my parents and most of our combined relatives.

We loved the tree-lined streets that led visitors into the downtown area where two state highways crossed, exposing the bank, the drugstores, family-owned general stores, furniture, and hardware stores. Everyone was proud that we had one of the largest hardwood lumber operations in the state and proud of the mini-industrial park that included factories that drew workers from surrounding communities. At the edge of northern Indiana's lake country, the rolling terrain of the surrounding farms was a pleasant contrast to the flat fields to the east and west. And while we didn't actually live in the town, preferring the country to any urban area, regardless of size, we liked the community and its people.

"It's going to be a big responsibility," I told Loren as we discussed plans over midnight tea and coffee.

His blue eyes snapped with enthusiasm. "You'd better believe it," he said. He'd already quit his job and was working at the paper, learning the operation of the presses, folder, caster, saw, router, strip caster, and all the other pieces of machinery used in a print shop. His vocabulary had become filled with strange new terms like coins, turtles, stones, and locking up. "You have to be careful when you lock up a form," he said. "You push on it and the type is pied all over the floor."

Piing is a printer's nightmare, the dreaded calamity that can result if a form is dropped or bumped as it is moved into place. But I was startled the morning he dashed back in the house and demanded, "Where's my make-up?"

"You gone funny on me?" I demanded as I rushed Todd out of the room so he couldn't hear his father.

"Don't be silly. This is a make-up," he said as he produced a thin piece of steel curved to fit neatly into his hand. It permitted him to lift slugs of type from galleys and, I was to learn later, it could be used as a screwdriver, a carton opener, nail cleaner—anything that demanded something either incredibly thin or strong for its size.

A dream had come true, a prayer had been answered. A camel caravan had been exchanged for a mailing list with slightly more than 1,000 names, a battered press, and a Linotype. Instead of becoming a correspondent who went to sea or to the desert, I was going to become a newspaperwoman, hopefully one who could be compared to the likes of Nellie Bly, Frances Wright, or Marguerite Higgins—but only on Thursday.

Owning the paper was my dream come true, but I was to have little to do with its actual operation. During one of our midnight tea and coffee sessions, it was decided that I should continue to work at the bank until we were more solvent financially. Still, I could be a viable part of the business by writing much of the news after work and especially by helping out on Thursdays. "You don't have to be there much the rest of the week," Loren said, "but you should make 'Always on Thursday' your motto."

"Isn't it wonderful that press day and my day off are both on Thursday?" I marveled. "What a coincidence."

"A coincidence is a gift to us from God," he said, and I nodded. We'd long ago agreed that God knows our wants and needs and supplies them accordingly. "We should never ask Him for anything, except maybe for strength," Loren said. "We should only give thanks." Again I nodded my agreement, afraid to admit I'd prayed hard for the paper since the day Russ set the process in motion. And who could say the prayers had not been answered? Here we were with no money, no experience, and a paper. The bank where I worked had loaned us the down payment, and the bank where I'd previously worked had loaned the balance. As far as I was concerned, this was a dream come true, answered prayer at its finest.

As August fog gave way to hot September days filled with

skittering grasshoppers, crickets, and gossamer, dew-sprinkled cobwebs in the grass, it was my turn to learn something of the newspaper business. During my Thursday afternoon introduction to journalism, I was given instructions on the operation of the mailing machine and a fifteen-minute cram session on how to compute legal advertising.

Now, with less than two hours of newspaper experience and a writing background that consisted of nothing but rejection slips, I was writing for publication, not just any publication but our very own newspaper. "Thank You, thank You, thank You," I whispered again as the Linotype operator snapped me out of my reverie by rattling the copy drawer in search of the next page of my story, a report of a meeting that eventually would do far more to change the community than anything so simple as our purchasing its seventy-two-year-old weekly newspaper.

The Indiana legislature had a few years earlier passed a bill that spelled doom for high schools the size Loren and I had attended. School consolidation, the bane of our grandparents' lives when one-room schools had been abandoned in favor of single township units, was again a reality. Only this time more was at stake than township lines. Many feared the actual life of the community was threatened, and emotions were heavily charged. Because our entire county had a population of slightly under 17,000, some favored a county school district. Others, however, feared the county seat would take charge and the smaller towns, such as ours, would lose their voice and with it any hope of continuing the comfortable, middle-class, predominately white, Anglo-Saxon, Protestant existence it had cherished for over 100 years. After a lengthy battle that resulted in new legislation permitting school corporations to be formed across county lines, four rural townships in two counties joined in a new school district. Affected were the schools in our town, another town ten miles to the north that was similar in size, and two schools that were even smaller, one in a town half the size of the other two and one in a community that in reality was only a school and a church. The prospect did not frighten me. Loren and I had grown up in one of the townships, I'd been born in another, and the other two seemed friendly. One of these was less than a mile from our home, and the township in which we lived would soon be the fifth to join the sprawling corporation. No conflict of interest there.

But there was a conflict of goals for the new school district, and at stake now were five seats on the new board. Twelve men had declared their candidacies. They had met the night before to air their views on the topic "What's Best For Our Children?" It was a heady subject, and their opinions were mixed. Now it was time for me to try to get them in order. No longer could there be procrastination because the windows were dirty or Todd wanted to play; the Linotype operator wanted copy, and he wanted it now. I had to produce.

I typed furiously, aware the press had stopped and Loren was filling other forms with type. The Linotype clattered and stopped, then started again as the operator cleaned up a spurt of molten metal and continued the laborious task of converting words into lines of type.

Tom Evans, as new to the business as we were, was clearly frightened as he continued to clean up the spurts. Sometimes he didn't duck in time and his arms gave testimony to the heat of the metal that bubbled over an open flame near his left hand. But he didn't hesitate. When a spurt ruined a line, he gamely grabbed a screw driver and forced the mangled slug from the machine, tossing it on a growing pile of scrap at the base of the Linotype. It was set, toss, set, toss for many months, but Tom never gave up. We rejoiced at his presence, which indeed seemed to prove Loren's conviction that God knew our needs and supplied them. We hadn't panicked when the country-trained operator who had worked for the previous owner hung up her apron on learning she soon would have a new boss. "Someone will come along," we said, and sure enough, here was Tom, young, energetic, willing, and armed with good recommendations from the school that had just graduated him.

To round out the staff, we had Peggy White, a vivacious widow who had worked for the previous owner as office manager and advertising representative, a role she was willing to continue for us. What more could we want? God had supplied everything.

Peggy grabbed the copy as fast as it came from my typewriter, full of typographical errors and misspellings, and rushed it to Tom who gamely set it into lines of type as he dodged the spurts. Loren snatched the lines as soon as they were cool enough to handle. This made Tom even more nervous, and the Linotype, a Rube Goldberg-type machine that weighed two-and-one-half tons and contained thousands of moving parts, clattered, balked, and squirted as he attempted to operate it at capacity.

Finally, the story was converted into type, and I heaved a sigh of relief as I saw Tom spindle the last sheet.

The relief was short-lived.

"Could you make up the front page?" Loren asked as he looked at the empty form in front of him and glanced again at the clock. He might as well have said, "Why don't you run to the moon and get me a sandwich?" but I said I guessed I could try. He tied an ink-soaked apron over my white blouse and handed me a make-up. "And here's the stick in case you want to set any headlines," he added.

I watched him go back to the press to take off the previous run and looked from the stick to him to the cases of handset type I'd so proudly showed friends on tours of the office and press room. This was going to be something else. I looked again at the type Tom had set. It was all upside down and backwards. I could read nothing. How could I put it in place when I couldn't read it? It was impossible. Or was it? I looked at the make-up in my hand and grinned. I knew the solution. I got out my makeup kit and held the mirrored compact over the lines of type. I could read every word now and while it was going to take a long time, I was confident I could make up the page.

"What are you doing?" Loren demanded as he returned from

the press. He took the mirror from me and said, "Just read the type the way it is. It's not that hard, and you might as well learn to do it right."

I prayed for help. God must have heard me because in spite of my hesitation, the page slowly began to take shape. In the process I learned Loren's kind of make-up was good for scraping excess metal off lines of type and for moving them from column to column. And with his help I managed to stick some type, putting into practice a method used for hundreds of years, although Benjamin Franklin and Mary Katherine Goddard would have been appalled to watch me plod my way one letter at a time, constantly referring to a wall chart. Good typesetters, I was told, became quite skilled in this ancient art and never needed to study a chart. They had had so much practice they could do it blindfolded. And good typesetters, I imagined, would not have used poster type for headlines, but perhaps they would have understood the pressure of a deadline passed and the sense of panic that accompanies it.

"There you go," I called to Loren as I finally stuffed the last line in place.

"Wheel the turtle over here," he called.

"The which?"

"The turtle," he replied, pointing to a cart with four wheels and a steel top.

"Why didn't you say so in the first place?" I muttered peevishly as I rolled the turtle into place and sighed. A camel caravan had been exchanged for a turtle. I sighed again. I was tired. After working at the bank all day Wednesday, I'd covered the meeting and then gone to the office to type copy before finally snatching three hours of troubled sleep. Loren had had even less, and his eyes showed fatigue. But we both knew a tradition rested on our shoulders. For nearly 73 years, area residents had known they could count on getting their paper every Thursday. Always on Thursday. We could not fail them by being the first to miss the final deadline.

Marveling at how much Loren had learned during that long, hot summer, I watched in fascination as he moved four forms of type onto the turtle and anchored them tightly together in a chase, using what he called a coin to ensure a safe hold. Actually spelled *quoin,* it was part of the strange new language he'd learned while I'd continued pursuing the world of debits and credits. "Can't lock it too tightly or it'll pi," he explained as I watched. "But if it's not locked tightly enough, it'll spill all over the turtle or the floor."

He pushed the turtle to the press and turned the chase on edge. I caught my breath as three hundred pounds of type and metal castings balanced precariously as he swung the chase to the bed of the press.

Like a child dreading a shot, I looked the other way, only daring to watch again after the chase was safely locked in place. "Thank You, thank You," I whispered repeatedly, although by now I felt like shouting it. There was going to be a lot more to newspapering than writing.

"I'll pull a proof," Loren said as he eased a sheet of paper through the press. The other pages had been his, but this run was mine because my first "live" story was on two of the four tabloid-sized pages printed on the single sheet of newsprint. There was no byline, nothing to tell the world it was mine, but my heart beat furiously.

"Ready to roll?" Loren yelled before Peggy and I had had time to read much more than the heavy, ultrabold headlines.

"Sure," I said as the huge press groaned into action.

"We didn't proof-read anything!" Peggy gasped.

"Is it very bad?" I asked, hating to admit I'd been so excited I'd barely skimmed the pages of print Loren handed us.

"It's pretty bad." My heart ached for her. The only member of the staff with experience, it had to be difficult for her to watch three beginners fumble and err.

"We don't have time to stop for corrections," Loren shouted over the din of the press. "We'll have to go the way it is."

Peggy gasped something that sounded like, "Heaven help us," as the two of us sat down to wait for the sheets to be turned, the time Loren would remove four printed pages from the stacker and return them to the feeder so they could be printed on the other side. As soon as a few came through the second time, he would cut them in half and it would be time for us to begin the laborious task of folding the pages, separating them and then collating them with the pages already printed, the ones Peggy had assembled and stacked in tall piles on an old golden oak library table that served as the mailing area. Lacking only a cover, our first paper was nearly complete, and I relaxed as I listened to the soothing sound of the press and watched the bed work back and forth as the cylinder spun off sheets of newsprint. Compared to the mimeograph machine we had used in high school, it seemed like nothing but a blur. I had nothing else to compare it with, but it certainly seemed like automation at its finest. I tried to forget that as recently as contract signing I had not known the difference between a press and a Linotype. I shuddered to realize that surely no one had ever wanted something so badly that she knew so little about.

"Fire!" Loren shouted and my reverie was broken. A page had misfed and caught in the gas burner designed to help eliminate static, a constant bogeyman in print shops. The top of the press was a sheet of flame. I froze in my tracks, scared to move, and wondered if my dream come true, my answered prayer, had just evaporated in a puff of smoke.

Tom jumped up from the Linotype and raced across the shop, a bucket of water in his hand. I never learned where he got it, but there was no doubt what he did with it. He threw it on the blazing press, and the fire fizzled out, leaving nothing but ashes and soot to show where it had been. The water stayed longer, dripping from the ink well and forming in puddles over much of the type. The stack of newsprint began to swell. Soon it was twice the size it had been when Loren put it in the feeder.

The telephone rang, and I heard Peggy say, "Yes, Hattie, the paper will be out today. We're just running a little late today. No problem."

Loren and Tom were removing the rollers from the press when the telephone rang again. This time it was my turn. "Yes, Sophie, the paper will be out today. You know you can depend on it—always on Thursday." By now the press had been completely stripped of its rollers and Loren and Tom were elbow deep in the ink well trying to blot out the water. I hated to tell Sophie I had no idea which Thursday it might be.

"Are Thursdays always bad?" I asked Peggy as we watched the men change newsprint and reassemble the press.

"Some are worse than others," she said, a reply that should have earned her the Understatement of the Year Award.

Finally the press groaned into action again, the run was turned, and Peggy and I could begin the final assembly. Was it just my imagination or did those papers really look wonderful as they were folded and counted into bundles for delivery to the post office and the grocery stores that would provide our newsstand sales? Just feeling the newsprint was a heady experience, one undiminished by the ink that rubbed off and soon covered my hands and arms.

I scooped up the piles and set off for the stores, my heart beating the same happy tune it had sounded all day. A dream had come true. A prayer had been answered. The first issue was off the press.

"How'd it go?" Ruby Pearl asked as I dashed into the Pearl Store, a general store selling everything from meat and potatoes to ready-to-wear clothes.

"Pretty good, I guess," I said. I didn't have time to go into details of the fire.

"You look awful."

"Really? I feel great. Absolutely exultant."

"Well, you look filthy. What have you done to yourself?"

I rushed to the mirror she kept behind the ladies' scarves and gloves and stared into a reflection I barely recognized. Ink was everywhere. My eyes were surrounded by a mask, created, no doubt, as I tried to rub sleep from them while assembling the papers. I had ink on my elbows and in my hair. My blouse, so crisp and white in the morning, had been reduced to a tattle-tale gray, a TV detergent huckster's dream.

"Maybe it'll get better," Ruby whispered. It was the first time I'd ever heard my boisterous friend so quiet, and it frightened me.

"I really look awful, don't I?"

"The first day is the worst."

The first day. Our first issue was out. It was in the mail. It was on newsstands. People would see it. Never mind how I looked, what about the newspaper we had just created? It was no longer ours. It belonged to everyone.

Waving an inky hand to Ruby, I rushed through the rest of my deliveries to retrieve Todd from his sitter. "What if no one likes it?" I asked myself a thousand times as I sped around town. "What right do we have to impose ourselves on others? What makes me think I can write? No one else ever thought I could except my mother and my English teachers. Oh my God, what have we done?"

"Let's get out of here. Let's get as far from town as we can," Loren said when I returned to the office. He was the picture of dejection. His face was as gray as the ashes that still clung to the press and his blue eyes were a bleary gray from lack of sleep.

"How far?" I asked, too weary to think of moving.

"As far as home. Right now—before anyone sees the paper."

I knew how he felt. Much as I longed to become an active part of the community, right then I wanted only to escape it, to flee, to regroup my thoughts, to reevaluate the paper.

"Does it help to know we aren't the first to feel like this?" I asked. "In his anniversary reminiscence, the founder of this paper said his first impulse was to run. He didn't even take his own papers to the post office. He sent the printer's devil."

"So did I, I guess," Loren said, his eyes taking in my inky appearance. "You're a mess."

"Thanks. I'll try to say something nice about you sometime," I muttered.

"I'd rather you found something decent to say about this week's paper," he groaned, staring at the front page.

With the deliveries out of the way, I took time to examine the front page closely for the first time. There were more typographical errors than most first-year typing teachers see on opening day of school. The page itself looked like a dowdy old lady with her slip showing. We'd followed a custom that had varied little in seventy-two years by putting deaths, personal items, and even the need for a new area correspondent on the front page. Not only did it fall far short of all established journalistic standards, it lacked even a single picture. The only photograph in the entire paper was a two-column wedding picture used on one of the first runs when type was scarce and the news hole gaping. No one had to read the masthead to know there was a new editor and publisher. Every page screamed *"Change of Ownership."*

"At least I don't have to come back tomorrow," I said as I looked at the scrambled type and realized a form did not have to be pied to become a jumbled mess. An inexperienced typesetter coupled with a novice in the make-up area could create equal results. I was suddenly very grateful for a job ten miles away. "Maybe if we go home and get a good night's sleep the thing will look better," I whispered.

"I doubt it," Loren said. "I just hope no one reads this week's paper."

But someone had read the paper, and before we could pull Todd from the pile of cast-off slugs that drew him like a magnet, Silas Monroe burst into the office. "Just wanted you to know I think your first issue is great. Good job. The Blabber never looked better."

"Are you kidding?" Loren asked, ignoring the older man's reference to the town's pet name for the *News*. But I could see a flash of blue as his eyes sparkled. "Thank you. Thanks for telling us."

"And thank You, God," I whispered.

"It'll be quite an education, newspapering will," Silas said. "It'll either make you alcoholics or religious fanatics."

"How's that?"

"Don't know how it happens, but I've seen newspapering do it to a lot of men. Gets to them after a while. Back when I was your age, if a newspaperman couldn't drink more booze, chew more tobacco, and chase more women than anybody else, he couldn't be editor. Those that didn't make the grade became religious fanatics."

"No middle-of-the-roaders?" I asked, rubbing at the ink spot on my elbow.

"It's pretty hard for an editor to hang in the middle. He has opinions, same as everyone else."

"We're just going to write it as it happens, whether it's a fender bender or a murder—or a drinking spree."

"Don't drink, do you?" Si asked.

"No."

"I see you at church a lot. How do you stand with it?"

"We go almost every Sunday. We're not very vocal people so you don't hear much out of us, but we have a good personal relationship with God."

"I'll bet all that changes in a couple of years."

"What—our not drinking or our relationship with God?"

"Either or both. You're going to change," he said as he ducked to avoid the front door that swung open to admit Hattie Hooper. "Newspapering does things to people."

"Well, it's not going to set these folks on the path to drink," Hattie said, looking Silas straight in the eye. Her dark hair was pulled back from her face so severely the hairline appeared in danger of becoming displaced from her scalp. Her black eyes snapped indignation. "Drinking's no good for anyone, newspaper people or you, Silas Monroe."

"It sure wasn't much good for Harry Hooper," Silas said as he watched Hattie leave with a paper in hand.

"Didn't he die when he fell down their basement steps?" I asked.

"Yeah, but he wouldn't have fallen if he hadn't been drunk as a skunk."

"No wonder Hattie hates liquor so much."

"Hattie's a good woman. She means well. She's trying to make up something to someone for Harry's death."

"She's a good Sunday school teacher," I said. "She taught my class, and she did a great job."

"None better," he agreed. "Just stay out of her way when she gets on the warpath about drinking."

The door swung open again, and Sophie Palmer popped into the room carrying a plate of cookies. "Thought you might be hungry after all that work," she said merrily, her snow white pompadour bobbing as she bustled from one to the other of us and flirted with Todd, still busily engaged under the Linotype. "But what was this I heard about drink? You got something to offer?"

"Nothing stronger than tea or coffee," I said.

"Shucks, I was hoping you might have a nip tucked back in the corner."

"How'd we get talking about drinking in the first place?" Loren demanded.

"Beats me. I just got here," Sophie said. "Personally, I think it's a good idea. A little drink never hurt anyone. Keep a bottle of whiskey at home all the time. Drink a teaspoon full of it every night before I go to bed. It keeps me healthy. If you ever hear that I died, you'll know my bottle ran dry."

"You're too mean to die," Silas teased.

"Betchyour life," Sophie snapped. "That's how I got to be so old. I always ran ahead of the pack. I never ate anyone's dust."

"You sure run a good boarding house," Si said. "I appreciate your giving a home to those boys I send you."

"You sure hire some characters down at your plant," Sophie

said, "but, really, most of them are pretty decent guys. They just need someone to look after them . . . mother them a little and give them a few suggestions."

"Better keep them out of your whiskey bottle."

"I'd break their arms if they touched it!"

"How are things at the Palmer House these days?"

"Oh, what you said!" she gasped, clapping ring-covered fingers to her mouth in mock horror. "Don't let those folks in Chicago hear you. They'll get me for pornographyism."

"I think the word's plagiarism," Silas said, his face crinkling into a broad grin he could no longer conceal behind his perennial scowl.

"Either way, they'd get mad at me. I got enough trouble right here with the likes of you."

Sophie and Silas left together, and Tom and Peggy burst into laughter.

"That's the way to get old," Tom said. He was almost as bleary as we were, but our town's senior citizens had brightened his day.

"You might as well get used to them," Peggy said. "They'll be here every Thursday to get the paper. They can't wait to get it out of their boxes at the post office. They want it while the ink's wet."

"How about Hattie?"

"Her too. Actually, she has a subscription because it's cheaper that way. But she comes here to pick up the paper. She doesn't want to miss anything. But don't sell her short. There's a lot more to that woman than meets the eye. She presents a steely exterior, but inside there beats a heart of gold. A Christian heart."

"You plan to change?" I asked Loren as we finally drove home.

"I think Silas was just exaggerating about newspapering changing people. I don't intend to change a bit. I plan to keep on farming in my spare time and operating the best print shop I can the rest of the time."

"Does that include putting out a good newspaper?" I asked.

"That has to include putting out a good newspaper. That's our business now."

"That's our business now." The words were as pleasing to the ear as "our own press," and I burrowed my face into our son's hair so Loren couldn't see my tears of joy.

"I've got it all," Loren said. "A wife, a son, a business of my own, a little farm. What more could a man want?"

"And I'm writing," I said as visions of camel caravans and dung fires gave way to the realities of scrambled type and a car filled with love. "God has been good to us."

"Super good."

We re-read the paper over pots of tea and coffee. It was a disaster. Misspelling followed typographical error, headlines were hyphenated and closer to full sentences than short capsulizations, and, worst of all, it was gray, gray, gray. "Gee, I hope no one sees it," Loren muttered for what seemed like at least the nine hundred and thirty-third time, and I miserably nodded agreement.

The telephone rang. It was Hattie. "Thought I'd tell you this week's paper's not too bad. If you learn to spell you'll have it made."

"Amen," I said.

A minute later the telephone jangled again. It was the editor of an area paper wondering if we cared if he quoted from our article about the school issue. "Go right ahead," I said, and days later I read their version of our story and hoped God would forgive me for laughing when I saw they'd copied all the mistakes, misspelling the same words and making the same transpositions.

All and all, fires and the Si and Sophie hour notwithstanding, it was a great beginning to an answered prayer. I whispered my thanks again and, unable to abide strictly by Loren's rule to limit prayers to thanksgiving, I prayed for God's help and guidance now and in the years ahead, every day and in every way, but especially on Thursdays. "Please, God, always on Thursday."

A lot of Thursdays had come and gone since that fateful day

the presses—or, more specifically, "our press," didn't stop, the day the camel caravan was traded for a turtle. There had been other fires, more scrambled type, and ink-soaked clothes. There had been tears and shouts of rage, but now in the warmth of our kitchen, we could reflect on the route our lives had taken in the past few years. Clearly, it was a journey even a camel caravan could not have duplicated. Often complicated and interwoven with deadlines and punctuated with squabbles, it was a route seldom boring. It was a seven-day journey that ended and began on Thursday. Always on Thursday.

3

Mussolini in the Bathroom

"What are you reading?" someone queried as we gathered for a late hour kaffee klatsch. The question didn't ask, "What newspaper or magazine do you read?" It wanted to know what book we were currently reading.

It's a question that always unnerves me, because I never know how to describe how I read books. How do I tell anyone I have them scattered all over the house? One in the living room, another in the bedroom, still another in the bathroom.

For instance, at a given time, I might be reading an anthology in the bathroom, short, easy-to-read things that don't detain me in what we've come to call the "family room." At the same time, my current favorite book, the one I read until I'm too sleepy to see, can be found in the living room. And on my nightstand will be still another book, one that doesn't require much concentration as I skim over a few pages each night.

"What are you reading, Ann?"

I stammered, "Well, it's kind of hard to describe." Now, my choice of reading might range from Guideposts in the bathroom to *The Image of Loveliness* by Joanne Wallace or a really good suspense novel in the living room to one of Marjorie Holmes' books in the bedroom. This particular time, however, I was reading a biography of Mussolini in the bathroom, a Victoria Holt Gothic in the living room, and Barbara Howar's *Laughing All The Way* in the bedroom. It was a very difficult combination to explain, and I hesitated.

"I'll bet it's something new you picked up at a meeting," Ruby said, her eyes sparkling with interest.

"No, not really," I said, starting to recite the books. "I'm reading Mussolini in the bathroom and . . ."

I got no further. Nancy Carter turned to Polly Wright and said, "The titles of these new books are disgusting. Imagine! *'Mussolini in the Bathroom!'*—that's going entirely too far! Isn't that invasion of privacy or something?"

I shrugged. After all, I'd warned them my reading was pretty hard to describe.

But if my reading was hard to delineate, what words do I use for the coterie gathering in my living room except to say we were a mixed group of individualists held together by one very strong and very important tie: We liked each other. And we still do.

Nancy Carter, the daughter of Hattie Hooper, was as petitely blond as her mother was large-boned and dark-haired, as quiet as her mother was outspoken. Hattie had been known on occasion to vent her impatience with sticky drawers, bent curtain hooks, and other household trivia by muttering "cheese and crackers" under her breath, but the strongest thing anyone ever heard Nancy say was, "Hmm."

Nancy and I were seniors the year her father slipped and fell to his death, but she never mentioned his alcoholism. Nor did her mother. "Hattie means little home ruler," she told our Sunday school class a week or so after Harry's death, "and I've ruled my home without liquor for nigh onto twenty-five years." There were a few snickers because everyone had heard about Harry's drinking bouts in the back of his appliance store. But no one ever heard Hattie mention Harry's drinking although nearly everyone came to hear how she'd ruled her home without liquor for thirty, forty, or fifty years.

After Nancy married Paul Carter they took over the management of Hooper's Sooper Appliance Store. "Dumb place will be called that till the end of time," Paul muttered every time anyone asked him when the name would be changed. "Old Hattie will never part with it. She's not about to sell it to me—not that I'd want the thing anyway. I'd rather be farming." Nancy worked side by side with Paul until the first of their three daughters was born. "A mother's place is in the home," she said as she withdrew to the cozy cottage Hattie fixed up for them across a narrow expanse of grass from her own home. Left on his own with a business he hated, Paul soon turned to Harry's favorite corner of the back room and began drinking. To his wife and family he presented a sober appearance, but sometimes it was two or three days between visits home. Nancy never complained. "Don't you worry when Paul doesn't come home?" we asked her at one of our kaffee klatches.

"No. Why?" she asked, startled. "I know where he is. If I needed him, I could reach him."

Complaining simply was not part of Nancy's lifestyle. "Sour grapes never gave anyone anything except a stomach ache," she said once when Polly complained that Willy was not affectionate enough. The strongest comment Nancy ever made was an occasional wistful suggestion that she wished Paul liked the appliance business a bit more. And we all knew she couldn't complain too much about the way he managed the store, because, in spite of his dislike for stoves and refrigerators, he was an excellent salesman who constantly won trips for two to foreign ports.

"I'd like to trade places with her just once," Polly said the day we waved good-bye to Nancy and Paul as they set off for Acapulco.

"You want to go to Mexico with Paul?" I teased, and Polly gave me a look that would kill.

"He's too hen-pecked for me and you know it. But just once, I wish Willy and I could go somewhere besides PTA meetings."

Tall, slender Polly, her light brown hair streaked with touches of blond, would never have the natural grace of Nancy. "But then not all of us are perfect size eights," she sighed. Polly, who must have been all of a ten, dieted constantly. "I have to stay slim for my career," she said. Her position as executive secretary for an attorney far outranked either Willy or their son, Willis Wright

III, known to everyone as Wee Willy.

Ruby Pearl hated her name. "Can you imagine a worse name?" she demanded as I passed cookies and poured more coffee. "It sounds like I should be a bawdy dancer instead of selling meat and potatoes. One jewel's enough, but then I had to go and marry Pearl. And some pearl he is," she grumbled good-naturedly as she looked into the den where our husbands were discussing school consolidation. "If he beefs to me one more time about how I keep the dresses in the clothing department, I'm going to bop him with a side of beef. I'd like to see him do any better. Maybe he'd like to try to keep those dresses sorted out after Patience Sandler gets through with them. She tries on everything we have in the store, then says, 'I'm afraid I'd better not get anything today. Everyone in town will have seen this dress, and they'll know where I got it.' "

"Probably Norman P. won't let her spend any money," Marty said. "He's a skinflint in spite of all his talk in church about how we should give, give, give until it hurts. The old tightwad's an anonymous donor so no one knows for sure if he ever contributes or not. All he does is make trouble, and I think he gives Patience more problems than anyone else."

"Unless it's us," Ruby snapped back. "We bought that store from him. 'Great up and coming business,' he told us. 'No way to go but up, and it's already the best store in town.' But when we sorted through all the stock we'd bought, most of it wasn't worth wearing to a dog fight. Who wants a blouse with the pocket off or a dress that has dots that polka faster than you can pick them off the floor? You wouldn't give it to your worst enemy, let alone try to sell it to your friends or anyone you'd want to come more than once. Norman P.'s a crook."

"He's a good promoter," I said, but I nearly choked on the words. I'd already had more than one encounter with the feisty Norman P. Sandler. ("The P. stands for Pious," Sophie Palmer told me, although I personally felt it stood for *Publicity.*) Norman P. Sandler was everywhere—he was active in church, but he was most active in arranging publicity for his pet projects, most of which centered around his latest endeavor, a line of fine saddles and bridles. "Norman P. Sandler, Purveyor of Fine Leather Goods," his sign read, but in reality he sold groceries and ready-to-wear on the side, running competition with Ruby and Jim in violation of his bill of sale.

"People just expect me to have those things when they come from horse shows," he said, but everyone knew he was selling to anyone, trucking merchandise to his shop from discount houses and inflating the prices. He counted on publicity to pull in the customers, not really caring if they had any interest in saddles or not. A sale was a sale was a sale as far as Norman P. was concerned.

But if Norman P. liked publicity for his store, he was a private individual otherwise. You would never find him on the town board or running for office. He preferred to pull strings from the sidelines, to manipulate his puppets to do his will. And puppets he had because of his wealth and his uncanny knack for getting publicity, but never through the local paper. "No one reads it," he said.

Norman P.'s specialty was starting newspapers, and he caused us a few sleepless nights by launching a free publication a week after we signed the contract for the *News*. But his paper had been short-lived, and we hoped its failure would discourage him from trying another, but it didn't. His desire for publicity was an insatiable craving that needed constant feeding. There had been other shoppers and radio programs based in his showroom, and once he even managed to get a daily to open a satellite office. Norman P. was not my favorite person, and I tried to steer the kaffee klatsch conversation to more pleasant topics.

"If you had one word of advice to give a newcomer in business, what would it be?" I asked Marty.

"Stay out of Norman P.'s way," she snapped.

"Other than that."

"I'd tell them that if they insisted on doing something as

stupid as buying their own business to watch out for the first three years. The first year most of all. It's the hardest and you'll go into the red, but the second year won't be quite so bad—you'll still be in the red, but you'll begin to see your way out. If you can hang on until the end of the third year, you should be okay because by that time you should start to show a profit."

Marty and Russ had owned the real estate business nearly three years, and it appeared to be following the pattern she outlined, although she had come to dislike the business intensely. She had enjoyed the freedom of having Russ on the road so much of the time, of being able to make her own decisions, to come and go as she pleased, to decide what clothes the children would wear. Russ had been home often enough to help with the major decisions, but the minor ones had been fun, and she resented having to share them. "Imagine having to ask, 'Do you think Susie should wear a dress or jeans to school today?' she complained. "I can make a few decisions. I don't need him to tell me what to do every day, and I certainly could get along without having to work in that office." Still, anyone who had crossed Russ had found Marty a difficult bear to pass. She had developed what Loren had come to call a "businesswoman's personality," that strange malady that often strikes "Ma" when "Pa" is unjustly attacked by a customer or a competitor.

We found truth in Marty's remarks. The first year had some bad Thursdays. There were fires and late papers, but we always printed on Thursday. Late on Thursday perhaps, but always on Thursday.

We added a new section for readers in a neighboring town, and I began a weekly column that sometimes ran every two weeks or every two months. It was one thing that gave me a feeling of being part of the paper as I continued working in the bank. I was the only teller in the county who spent her day off hoisting forms of type, learning to make up pages, and mastering a strange new vocabulary. It was an exciting, busy year for all of us. Todd was a busy kindergartener with new friends and varied interests. All we needed to make our lives complete was another child and for me to join the staff on a full-time basis.

I was well into my seventh month of preparing for one of those events when the telephone rang one busy Thursday and we learned the only other newspaper in the school corporation was for sale. "It would be a good idea for one publisher to own both papers," the caller suggested.

The idea was staggering. Two papers instead of one. Already deeply entrenched in school consolidation in which our district found itself faced with the question "One or two?" in regard to the number of high schools it should maintain, we now found ourselves faced with a similar decision.

"What'll we do?" we asked each other, and the answer was always the same: Think about it. Pray.

We thought. We prayed. We asked other people.

"Don't eat anyone's dust," Sophie Palmer said.

"Can you handle it?" Silas Monroe asked.

We took stock of our situation. We already worked all night every Wednesday to meet one deadline. The second paper would mean a lot of Tuesday midnight oil. But we were young. That should help. But what of the baby coming "sometime in February, March or April," according to the doctor's calculations? It was already February. If we bought the paper we would have to hire more help.

I suspect Loren probably thanked God for the opportunity, but I was more definite, but not as definite as the first time. "If it be Thy will, help us buy it," I prayed. I felt nothing. I figured I'd kept God so busy with other prayers, especially on Thursday, that He didn't have time for more. We decided to make the plunge.

Editors and publishers of not one but two weekly newspapers—my dream had come true and was multiplying faster than I was. I chafed at my inability to work in both towns, the one we knew so well that most residents could tick off our combined genealogies over a cup of coffee, and the other that we knew only because it was in the same school district.

Still, the other town was not unlike our own, I discovered as I waddled from store to shop to office on my first visit, finding to my surprise that Ruby, Polly, Nancy, and Marty were there, too. And I met Hattie Hooper, Sophie Palmer, and had tea with Silas Monroe.

Norman P. Sandler was there, too. Unhappy about the sale of the paper to "those people from the other town," he started a shopper devoted strictly to his town. "We don't need to read about anyone else," he told the Chamber of Commerce when he introduced the out of town people who would print the paper. "What we need is a lot of publicity about our town."

And then I knew why there had been no easy answers to our prayers. We had turned the pages of progress back to day one, page two. On Marty's schedule, we had just lost nearly two years. We were starting over.

Norman P. and his insatiable demands for publicity revealed all too clearly that country journalism is not the same as camel caravan reporting, that in the final analysis no one really cares if someone writes a book about Mussolini in the bathroom. As long as it's not his ox being gored, a Norman P. Sandler doesn't care what Mussolini does, nor does he care if news of Norman P. Sandler, Purveyor of Fine Leather Goods, is read in the bathroom. He just wants it read, locally, of course, but not as locally as the weekly newspaper. That's too local. Everyone here knows him. But he doesn't want to read what his namesake in another town is doing. That'd be like actually knowing what Mussolini did in the bathroom.

I prayed for strength to live with my answered prayers.

4

Two Instead of One

I was a very pregnant participant in an entirely new ball game. And while I couldn't spend much time in our newest office, I could at least try to get acquainted. When a club invited me to attend a meeting, I jumped at the opportunity, dressing with care and hoping my smock top would conceal my condition while I prayed my nerves would not betray me. The nerves won. As I lumbered up the steps, I tripped and literally fell into the meeting head first. Frightened and confused, I sat on the floor as blood poured from a knee that had not looked like that since I was six and fell trying to roller skate. What had been a new pair of hose hung in shreds. Still, I realized as I eased my bulk onto a folding chair, no one needed to wonder what I looked like. I was very, very visible, the woman with the bloody knee, that huge, huge woman who sat frozen in her chair for fear the fall would cause her to go into labor before the secretary read the minutes.

The fall didn't cause the baby to come early, and it was a good thing, because there were too many things to do, not the least of which was to find help for Loren. He simply couldn't handle all those press runs, especially without someone to make up pages for him, and we both knew that shortly he would have to take over that job at least for the time I was in the hospital.

We inserted a "help wanted" ad in the *News* and got only one applicant, Sonny Sandler, son of Norman P. and Patience.

Sonny had been in our class in school, and I remembered him

43

as the curly-haired little boy who still wet his pants in fifth grade, who ran home crying to his mother when the teacher demanded he have his papers turned in on time. Loren and I had attended one of his three weddings. We had seen him often enough since he returned to live with his parents after his last divorce to know he had none of his father's drive, little of his enthusiasm, and none of his desire for publicity. He made the latter amply clear the day he stormed into the office and said, "You know I hate publicity. Why did you feel compelled to print the dumb news about my drunken driving arrest? You know I can't stand my name in print."

"You were arrested, weren't you?" Loren asked.

"That has nothing to do with it," Sonny whined. "You just shouldn't put that kind of news in. Just print good news."

Norman P. had been more direct. "You crucified my son," he snapped. "You actually went out and crucified him in print." In retaliation, he withdrew his weekly classified, a three-dollar a month loss of revenue.

It wasn't a very good recommendation for hiring, but we were desperate. My due date was getting closer, and we were getting further and further behind. I didn't see how I could possibly take off a minute to have a baby, let alone a week or two.

"Maybe Norman P. will advertise more if we hire Sonny," Loren said over tea and coffee.

"It's worth a try," I agreed, not realizing we were unwittingly committing a cardinal sin in our desperation. You don't hire relatives of business associates, your own relatives, or relatives of someone whose friendship or advertising dollars you hope to cultivate. They're all destined for failure.

We hired Sonny, learning to our surprise that he had once worked for one of the papers his father had launched, and he knew the basics of presses and Linotypes. "But he's sick a lot," we were warned. So he's sick a lot, we reasoned. If he knows how to operate a press, he'll be an asset. We called him and told him the job was his.

"I'm not feeling very well today, but I think I can make it tomorrow," he said.

"Yech," Loren said, but both of us were pleasantly surprised the next morning when Sonny reported for work bright and early. And we beamed happily as he coaxed the ancient press into action, deftly catching sheets that misfed.

"This may work out yet," I whispered just as I heard the press groan to a halt and saw Sonny wander off in search of a soft drink. He'd just eaten a candy bar and the area behind the press was lined with empty pop bottles. "He's a frail boy," Patience had told us. "Can't eat sugar. Not cane sugar anyway. I have to use beet sugar for everything he eats." We wondered if Patience knew Sonny also had the biggest sweet tooth in town. We never saw him eat a bite of solid food. He refused offers of sandwiches with a shrug. "Can't eat them. I'm allergic to meat." But he could make short work of bags of junk food.

Gradually, we adjusted ourselves to Sonny's erratic eating habits, his constant desire for sweets, and we figured if he could keep the press running he should be allowed a snack or two. But we wished he wouldn't shut off the press to eat. Deadlines had to be kept regardless of cravings.

"Where are you going?" we asked late one afternoon as the press shuddered to a stop and Sonny headed towards the door. The candy and soft drink supply was in the opposite direction, and there were now two deadlines to be met, the first already past. We could only wonder when the second would be met.

"I'm tired. Think I'd better rest up for a day or two," he answered.

Furiously, I stamped in front of him and blocked his path. "Listen here, Sonny, we've got to have some help we can depend on. Loren can't work all night every night; he has to have someone he can count on to run that press. And in case you don't know it, I'm going to have a baby. I can't make up pages while I'm in the hospital. Either you or Loren will have to do that while the other runs the press. Tom's busy with the Linotype. You can't

expect him to do it. You may feel tired, but you've only been
here three hours and in that time you've had the strength to eat a
dozen candy bars and drink a six-pack of pop. You'd jolly well
better get used to working and you'd better be here when the
time comes for me to have this baby, because Old Mother Nature
is one person who doesn't wait for sweet breaks."

I went home and cried. Never in my life had I talked like that
to anyone, and I wasn't proud of the way I'd shouted at Sonny.
But there were two deadlines to be met, and I didn't like the way
Loren's face was becoming haggard and lined, the way silver was
crowding out the bright red of his hair. And I certainly didn't
like to see him so tired the blue of his eyes drained away and was
replaced by solid gray. I worked as late on Wednesday nights as I
could, sometimes spending part of the night on a cot while Todd
stayed with my parents. Other nights I went home at 3 A.M. and
toppled into bed too tired to care if I had the baby that night or
not. It was not the prenatal care recommended by Dr. Spock.
Clearly, I was showing signs of what Loren called Marty's businesswoman's personality, and the thought was frightening.

I was afraid to see Loren, but to my surprise he was home early
and he was smiling. "You're not angry?" I whispered as I tried to
blink back hot tears.

"No. A little surprised, maybe, but certainly not angry. I just
didn't know you had it in you."

"But I shouldn't have shouted at him."

"He had it coming."

"Do you think he'll quit?"

"Probably."

"Don't you care?"

"Like you told him, Mother Nature doesn't wait."

"What'll we do?"

"Everything's worked out okay so far, hasn't it? Just take it
easy, something will happen. God won't let us down now."

The something that happened was what we expected. Patience
called early the next morning to tell us Sonny would no longer be

with us, that he had felt ill all night and was still in bed. Norman P. called an hour later and canceled his classified ad, the one he had decided to rerun after we'd hired his son. "I'm very disappointed with you," he said. "A true Christian never shouts."

Our balance sheet was so precarious we knew we'd miss even the three-dollar a month loss of revenue, but we sent Sonny his paycheck and prayed for help. But the God who never failed us, the one Paul told the Corinthians would never suffer them to be tempted above what they were able but with the temptation would also make a way to escape, didn't need to hear any anguished pleas from us. He sent us a fine, young, Christian man with a growing family. Dick wanted to earn a little more income than his present job afforded, and he was willing to moonlight by working on the press two days a week.

With the press in conscientious hands, I was relieved of my composition duties by Loren and was free to turn my energies to editing, a role I'd long sought and now pursued with vigor, chafing when correspondents turned in sloppy copy or didn't produce enough.

"I'm going to mark this baby," I growled to myself as I raced up and down the highway to get copy from the two offices. "No one should be as angry as I've been lately. The baby is going to have a vile temper if I don't slow down."

Though we were still novices, we demanded perfection, from ourselves and from everyone who worked for us. We got it from no one because we really didn't know what we wanted. We wanted our two publications to become professional looking, preferably overnight, but we had little idea of how to achieve the results we sought. Our goals were continually redefined at midnight tea and coffee sessions but seldom communicated to the staff.

But we were determined not to give up. Bulldog determination would see us through, correspondents or Norman P. Sandler or anyone else notwithstanding. We just decided the papers would grow and be good. Period. But we didn't stop praying. I don't know how Loren prayed, but I asked God to make me tougher than anyone else.

More times than I care to remember, I stormed into one of the offices and thrust a spindle full of copy into the faces of one of the employees and snapped, "Look at that! You see that—that's what I did today. What did you do?"

"If we didn't need help so badly, I'd fire you on the spot," I'd shout when someone handed me two pages of news that would have to be redone if we didn't want to go into print saying the bride was attired in a yellow rose corsage. No mention of clothing, just a corsage.

Raging from one office to another, I seldom gave any thought to the "people person" who was becoming more and more a tyrant on wheels with a thirty-mile area as her beat and whose writing consisted of little except rewrites. My prayer had been answered, but my actions had tarnished it a bit.

But it was time for another prayer to be answered, and as I careened down the road in Loren's truck, clutching the wheel tightly as I took bumps too hard, I could no longer ignore the pains that wracked my body. "Dropping pains. They'll go away," I reasoned as I ignored a "Rough Bridge" sign and hit an approach at sixty miles an hour. I was too furious to use any caution, too intent on the meeting that loomed ahead that night, one that would be followed by an all-night session at the office, to slow down. The pain gripped harder.

By the time Loren came home for supper I was calmer but the pains were stronger, and I called my apologies to the chairman of the meeting.

"You'd better plan to get along without me tonight," I told Loren. "These dropping pains are awful."

"You're certain they're dropping pains?"

"We don't have time for any other kind," I replied.

"What was that speech about Mother Nature again?"

"What I'm really saying is that there's no way I want to have a baby on Tuesday night and let all the other papers scoop us before

we come out on Thursday," I said, wishing he would go back to
work and leave me alone.

"If you need me, call," he said, and I wondered if all my
thoughts were that easily interpreted.

By midnight, I had to give in and call him. We dropped Todd
off with his aunt and uncle and raced to the hospital, certain we
had only minutes to spare. "You still want to wait until Thursday?" Loren teased as we entered the hospital.

"If the baby's born tomorrow, no one will believe you when
you go to work. It's April Fool's day."

But there was no need to worry. The baby was in no hurry.

"It's supposed to be a girl," I told the nurse who volunteered
to sit with me after Loren gave up and went back to the office.

By the time Loren returned the next morning I was too tired to
care what we had. The baby was being very stubborn. But I was
happy to see my mate didn't look too grim. Dick, the new
pressman, was working out fine although he'd just recently had
the distinction of being the first person ever to pi a form on press
day. And Beulah, our slowest correspondent, had gotten her copy
there on time. It was a pair of small miracles, and we were
grateful.

But the miracle of birth we had waited for so long was slow in
arriving. We'd been married almost eleven years. Maybe we
shouldn't have waited so long to start our family, or to finish it.
Maybe our priorities were scrambled. A lot of frightening
thoughts churned through my mind as I labored on through the
second night and into the next day. Something was wrong. For
almost thirty years my life had unfolded the way I wanted it—
high school, college, marriage, living in Europe, a son, a newspaper of our own. A second child, the one we'd kept postponing,
was all we needed to make our lives complete. God had answered
so many prayers, it didn't seem fair to bombard Him with more,
but I prayed constantly that the baby would be all right. I
couldn't bring myself to ask for help for my misery. I wept
instead.

But suddenly, miraculously, after two days of labor, the baby arrived, all eight pounds, three ounces of him. So not all dreams come true, the girl was a boy, a chubby, red-headed boy. I was never so happy in my life. Two sons. The idea didn't sound all that bad. In fact, it seemed just perfect, and I whispered, "Thank You, thank You, thank You," over and over as I watched the doctor and nurses work. And when I heard a nurse whisper, "Look at his big nose," and the doctor reply, "Sshh, look at his mother's," I laughed. It was like a re-run as I remembered how the German doctor had looked from me to my first-born and said, "Di Nase de same."

But all was not the same. Doug required several whacks from the doctor before he shrieked his protest at the world; Todd had arrived howling. Maybe I've had a quieter baby, I thought as I looked at the plump infant the nurse cradled in her arms.

As the nurse carried Doug away, the doctor said, "I want to show you something, Ann." His voice sounded serious as he pulled the birth cord from a pan. "See this knot. If it had been any tighter, the baby would have been dead."

"What caused it? My falling? My lack of patience with the world lately? All the racing around I did while I carried him?" The thought that I might have endangered our child chilled me to the bone.

"The fall maybe. Who knows. It's one of those things that happens sometimes. I just wanted you to know you came awfully close to losing this little fellow."

"Nothing to worry about later on?"

"It's too early to tell yet, but I doubt it." His words were reassuring, and I thanked God for this quiet, dedicated physician who never became excited, who had interrupted his day off to deliver our son, who even now was dressed for a tramp through the woods in search of elusive spring morels. "But," he said, "if you want another baby, for heaven's sake don't wait another six years. You're getting too old for this kind of thing."

"We've always wanted just two," I replied, putting out of my mind a scene that would be indelibly stamped there years later.

Suddenly remembering we were now two instead of one in more ways than one, I sat up on the delivery table and shouted, "Call Loren! It's only 11:30! We can still make this week's paper!"

"Newspaperwomen!" the doctor muttered, but he gave instructions to an aide, and within the hour Hattie, Silas, and Sophie were reading of the birth of Douglas Brian Sheetz.

"Some people will do anything for a scoop," Loren teased when he came to see his second-born for the first time.

"Almost anything," I corrected.

"What do you mean?"

"I mean let the community debate whether one is better than two. For us two is best. Two sons. Two papers. That's enough for anyone."

5

Growing Pains

"**W**hat this place needs is more help," Orlando Q. Blythe said as he dropped off a story about his lodge. "Why don't you hire a bunch of teen-agers to help assemble the paper every week. No sense you people standing there when those kids could do it just as well. They need something to keep them off the street."

"Good idea," Loren agreed. "We might be able to have them assemble your lodge bulletin, too."

"Good grief, no!" Orlando sputtered. "I want someone we can depend on to get the job done."

"But you said they needed work."

"They'd probably work good enough for a weekly newspaper. Past that I don't think I'd count on them."

"Good enough for a weekly newspaper." It was a comment we would hear often, a comment that never failed to make tempers flare at the insinuation that weeklies amounted to little, tempers that had to be restrained for fear of irritating advertisers, employees, or readers. We couldn't risk losing another Sonny Sandler and/or his father. We could only smile at Orlando's suggestion and go on publishing weekly newspapers. They were our way of life now, and, in spite of my hospital vow, two was not enough. We could not stop with two papers any easier than we could eat only one peanut. One called for another. Newsprint crowded the building and printer's ink permeated our clothes and filtered into our veins as we added other publications designed to underwrite losses on the first two, publications that would keep the press busy, a press now presided over by Pete, a full-time employee who had replaced Dick. We had hated to see Dick go; he'd been a good worker, a calming influence in a shop often made hectic by Thursday fires and twice-a-week deadlines. But we could understand his need for more rest. It was a need we often felt ourselves but seldom seemed to satisfy.

Pete's salary threatened to again put us back to the beginning of the first year on Marty's timetable, a spot we'd barely budged from since adding the second paper, but we hoped it would be justified by improved production. We would have to keep the press busy to meet the payroll. In order to meet the payroll we'd have to have another Linotype because Tom, whose skill increased daily, simply could not produce enough type to keep the press busy. This caused us to hire other part-time people, both in the office and in the shop. And the second Linotype meant other payments to be met. It was a vicious cycle, one that kept us racing even more frantically to meet not one or two deadlines but four.

Four deadlines, three each week, one once a month. Four newspapers. Four mastheads, four flags, four sets of interests. And three editors. The building fairly exploded with activity—our two weekly newspapers were sandwiched between a weekly published by a man long on enthusiasm and short on cash who had been convinced by his town's Norman P. Sandler to start a paper just for "us," and a monthly publication published by Orlando Q. Blythe's lodge.

But we weren't complaining. Beulah had been replaced by Paula who had no objections to turning in her copy on time, who didn't mind updating the mailing list. We took Orlando's advice and hired a group of teenagers to fold and assemble papers as they came from the press, coming to look forward to the weekly invasion of the shop by Debbie, Cindy, Holly, and Jackie who regaled us with tales of teacher atrocities and an inedible item on the lunchroom menu: rubber witches, which were called grilled cheese sandwiches by the cooks who didn't appreciate the humor of the nickname in spite of their acknowledgment that the sandwiches did bounce when they got cold.

But sandwiches that bounced, either on plates or off the walls, were far from the minds of Hattie Hooper, Vera Ross, Cora Jones, Ivy Marshall, and Nettie Nelson, the hard-working widows who filled the shop once a month to help mail Orlando Q. Blythe's lodge bulletin.

Hattie, always immaculate with her tightly drawn hair and starched housedresses, was a good worker, one who cheerfully headed up the mailing staff. She was never rattled by the demands of the other women, women as fluffy and light-headed, as she called them, as Vera Ross and Cora Jones.

Vera was one of our local news correspondents, one who seldom complained about our editing her copy. She just turned it in and enjoyed seeing her name in print. Hearing the hum of activity in the shop one day as she left her news, she stuck her head around the corner and asked, "What's going on?"

"Mailing day," Hattie replied.

"Care if I stay?"

"Always need more help," Loren answered as he carried another stack of papers to the table where the women worked.

Vera proved to be a cheerful worker, one who liked to joke she'd only been out of state once when she went with her late husband Orville to visit a friend in Michigan City. But even if she had never been past the state line, her world was big enough to include a host of friends and relatives, all of whom loved to visit her because she was such a good cook and so much fun to be with. Not more than five feet tall, she was round as a globe with funny little legs that looked like Tinker Toys beneath her favorite purple dresses.

Cora, slightly younger than the others, was also a bit more garrulous, her remarks often dripping acid. "Don't pay her any mind," Sophie said. "She's a good enough person underneath."

But we wondered if we'd ever really see past the bright layer of makeup that covered her gruff exterior. Nor could we understand why she had come to work for us. Certainly our first meeting had left something to be desired. Who could forget the Thursday evening she burst into the office waving her copy of the *News,* shouting, "What did you do to my club's news item?"

"Edited it," I said meekly, remembering the crop of commas that had burst from it, the first person pronouns, the ending that said, "A delightful time was had by all and refreshments were served on dainty plates."

"I feel like the arms and legs have been torn off my baby. You've thrown it in the street for everyone to see. It's terrible." Her eyes flashed angrily behind the makeup as her frosted wig slowly settled over her forehead.

I tried to show her why each change had been made, but she was heartsick. "Lettie's Haviland *is* dainty. The refreshments *were* good. Everyone *did* have a delightful time."

"People just don't have time or really want to read that kind of thing any more."

"My baby, my beautiful baby," she kept moaning as her wig sank closer and closer to her arched brows. "Dead for all the world to see. God'll get you for this. You should print it like I wrote it."

But by the next week Cora had joined the mailing staff. It was a paradox we couldn't understand, nor did we care to. She was a good worker, and we found the caustic comments added a light touch to a mailing area crowded by five widows and all the brethren from his lodge that Orlando could squeeze into his friend Lloyd's van.

Even printing Orlando's bulletin was as big a paradox as Cora's coming to work for us. In fact, our first encounter with Orlando had been even worse than our meeting with Cora. He had submitted a poem to us with the expectation we would pay him for it. We never used poetry and we couldn't afford to pay the kind of rates he had in mind. I wrote what I felt was a polite note explaining why I was rejecting the material and suggested he send it to a magazine rather than to a newspaper. Most novice writers would have let it go at that, but not Orlando Q. Blythe. The next thing I knew, a tall man, elegant in his stiffly dated Sunday best, his hair a wreath of snow white above his lined face, was leaning over my desk, waving his finger under my nose shouting, "I received your 'friendly' and laconic notation to submit my poem to a magazine. Your excuse was very poor. It's obvious you do not like to do a writer any favor."

"Any favor?" I gasped, remembering all the rejections I had received over the years, none of them as friendly as the one I had sent Orlando.

"You'd better search your heart and see if you can find the real reason for your lack of interest. I'll bet you're parsimonious."

"Never did care for parsnips," I heard Sophie's voice chatter from the shop where she was dispensing cookies, but Orlando pretended not to hear.

"If any great literary success should ever come my way, I am quite certain that I won't blame you for it." With that Orlando stormed out of the office. I'd never seen him before and I didn't suppose I'd ever see him again, but within a week he stopped by to see if we'd let him bring in his lodge news.

"Sure," we said. "We like all the local news we can get."

"Might as well have you publish the lodge's bulletin, too," he said. "Last printer got tired of it. Said it cost too much to put it out for what we could pay."

"I think we can make it on what you offered," Loren said in a sweeping statement that carried us into additional tons of newsprint and more new employees, most of whom reported for work only on mailing days and often carrying plates of candy, cookies, and doughnuts.

Mailing days were fun days. Food and coffee flowed freely. And advice. "Now Orlando, if I were you, I'd tell that daughter of yours to keep her kids home more."

"That's what I should do, Hattie," Orlando would agree, "but it'd be about as hard for me to tell her that as for you to tell Nancy that Paul shouldn't spend so much time in the back room."

"He's not Harry, that's for sure."

"He's going to be unless something happens."

"Anybody for more cookies?" It was Sophie Palmer to the rescue again. Every shop needs a Sophie. Every town needs a Sophie. Alert, interested, a busybody kept busy with work, a keen sense of humor, and the discernment to know when a conversation has gone too far.

The shop hummed with activity sometimes broken by fires or spurts on the Linotypes, but it was a good sound, and we rejoiced. God had answered thousands of prayers, spoken and unspoken.

At home, things were progressing equally well. Doug had arrived with no real plans made for his care; we had simply trusted God would find a good sitter, and we felt rewarded when Alma came. Actually, she applied as a proof reader. "I thought you might need someone since there are so many mistakes in the paper," she said shyly.

"Not really," we replied, much to her amazement. "What we really need is a baby sitter."

"Oh, I can do that, too," she said. And she did, cheerfully caring for Doug, marveling with us at our active youngster with the bright red hair and impish brown eyes. She sterilized the equipment used for his formulas so well the markings disappeared forever from the measuring cups, but she still had time to read and play games with Todd. We were off to a busy new beginning, and it was going to be good. Two sons instead of one, two newspapers instead of one.

We were certain there would be growing pains, and there were. It was impossible to print two newspapers in the same school district without ruffling tempers, without irritating chambers of commerce or the school board. The one-or-two-school question was still a meaty bone of contention. The final count would not be reached locally for many years and until it was we would remain the paper dragon, very visible and very vulnerable.

But there were other pains, very real pains, and they doubled Loren up as he tried to lift a form onto the press. "Probably from all those plums you ate," I said unsympathetically, looking at the empty bag that an hour earlier had been filled with fresh fruit.

He managed to make it through most of the run, but he finally asked Pete to take over and went home. He must really be sick to go home before we're done, I thought, but I helped finish the mailing before I went to check on him. He was the sickest I'd ever seen him.

"It's just a stomach ache," he gasped, his face contorted with pain. "It'll go away."

But it didn't go away. The pain became so intense he finally yielded to my pleas that he at least get a medical opinion.

"He's awfully sick, but I think he just has a touch of the flu," the doctor said when I pounded on the door of his home long after office hours and pointed to my husband clutching a dishpan as he sat doubled over and retching in the front seat. He poked Loren's stomach a couple of times and sent us home with the admonishment, "Keep an eye on him."

Keeping an eye on him wasn't hard. He seldom moved off the couch. Todd and I alternated shuttle duty with the dishpan and kept the baby away from him. We didn't need two victims of the flu bug. And for good measure, to keep him comfortable, I let him curl up with a heating pad and wrapped him in an electric blanket with the control set on high.

"All that heat helped," he said the next morning. "I felt a big sense of relief in the middle of the night." But he didn't feel like going to work, a very unusual thing for my workaholic mate. I went without him, leaving my three men in the care of one dubious baby sitter.

To my surprise, Loren actually went back to the doctor. This was a first. The man who fought going to a doctor harder than Muhammad Ali can punch had actually gone on his own. "I feel better," he said when he called to report. "The only trouble I had getting there was lifting my foot to put my pants on. I couldn't move it."

"You're just drained from being sick," I said and, remembering a party that night that would be attended by all the girls in our high school graduating class, I added, "You want me to stay home this evening?"

"No need for that," he replied cheerfully. "Go ahead and tell them all 'hi' for me."

"Did the doctor say anything else?"

"He suggested maybe I should drop by the hospital for some tests."

"What kind of tests?"

"Blood tests or something. I don't know. I do feel better, though, so don't worry about me."

Reluctant to take too many chances, I hired Holly, one of the part-time school girls, to stay with the boys and Loren while I went to the party. I had already fallen into a routine that would seldom vary in the years to come: Nothing, sickness or bad weather, would prevent my attending a meeting I'd marked on my agenda.

The party was fun and reminiscences were many, but the night grew dark and stormy. The wind whipped white caps across the lake our classmate's house faced. With each new gale I felt a stronger urge to be home with the sick, to be somewhere that wasn't on the agenda. A window shattered and blew across the living room, and we raced to cover the opening. The lights went out and we lighted candles. It was a night that portended turmoil, and I prayed the roads would still be open when the storm stopped.

"Are you okay?" I asked hours later as I dashed into the house, having skirted fallen trees and power lines to return home.

"Sure," Loren said, but I didn't believe him.

"He doesn't look right," Holly whispered.

"He's too red even for a redhead."

"He's fine!" Loren shouted, but we ignored him, and I asked Holly to come back the next day "just in case the doctor finds something when he runs the tests."

By morning, my ailing spouse seemed to feel better but he let me drive, and he complained all the way to the hospital that I hit bumps much too hard.

"Why do you keep holding your belt away from your stomach?" I asked.

"Feels better that way."

Our doctor was joined by one of his colleagues in examining Loren, and neither seemed to think anything very serious was the matter. "We'll do blood tests just to be sure," one of them decided. Loren and I sat in the lobby waiting for the results. While we waited we planned the week ahead and how we would cope with all the meetings to be attended and all the reports that had to be written. And we could only speculate what Norman P. Sandler might want at a meeting he had scheduled for some of the businessmen.

Our planning session was interrupted by one of the doctors who rushed to my side and shouted, "You'd better admit him right away." The other doctor was already pushing a cart to where we sat.

"What's wrong?" I asked.

"Appendicitis. It's hot and we're going to do emergency surgery right now."

Oh well, it's Saturday, I thought as I fumbled with dates and hospitalization insurance forms. He should feel well enough to be back by the middle of next week. He can at least boss the rest of us.

I dashed back down the hall just as the cart carrying Loren was pushed into the surgical suite. He sat up and shouted, "The front page goes on the northwest corner of the turtle." The doctors looked startled, but I knew I had my marching orders.

As with Doug's birth, Loren's surgery took too long. "An appendectomy can't take that long," I muttered as I watched minutes stretch into hours. I called the sitter and gave her new instructions, and I called my mother with instructions for formula in case I wasn't home in time. And I prayed for strength for all of us.

Hours later, the team of doctors, actually the last two of the county's old-time physicians, twenty-four-hour-a-day country doctors who pulled no punches, met me in the lobby. "Come on in, Ann, we have to show you something." I'd heard that expression before, but it still sounded ominous. I followed them into a small room where they handed me a jar with a large organ in it.

"Is that the appendix?" I asked.

"Yeah. And look at it."

I looked, but it didn't look very great to me.

"It's ruptured. As soon as we made the incision, fluid sprayed out. He's going to be an awfully sick man for a long time."

I felt myself go pale. Our landlord in Germany had been a walking skeleton the entire time we lived there because his appendix had ruptured the previous year. What would I do if Loren took that long to recuperate?

"He should be dead," one of them was saying, "but we think he's going to be all right. He just didn't have the right symptoms."

"How long has it been ruptured?"

"Probably since Thursday night."

"That's when he felt so much relief after I wrapped him in the electric blanket," I whispered.

"You sure cooked it," they agreed, and I wanted to scream, "But I thought he had flu—I only did what I thought was right." But I only asked to see Loren, whispering silent thank yous and fighting back tears.

They led me to the recovery room where a nurse was monitoring Loren's pulse and attempting to hold his intravenous tubes in place as he tossed and turned as the anesthetic wore off. She looked puzzled. "He keeps saying something about turtles," she said.

"He likes turtles?" one of the doctors asked.

"Just one kind," I replied as I left to call more orders to my parents and the sitter and to reassure Todd his father would eventually be all right. I called Norman P. Sandler and told him Loren would be unable to attend his meeting.

"Why?"

"He's just had emergency surgery. He's full of tubes and IVs and will be for at least a week."

"You mean he can't come to the meeting?"

I wanted to scream, "You idiot, why do you think I called? How do you think a man looks after he's had surgery?" but I bit my tongue and said no, I guessed he wouldn't be there, knowing without asking that another of Norman P.'s publicity gimmicks would be in the mail before Loren was dismissed. And then I went home and counted my blessings: one sick but very much alive husband; two sons, one only three months old; a farm and two newspapers except the times there were four. God had answered our prayers abundantly, and all I could do now was whisper, "Please help me, God. Help me get through the next few weeks. Give me the strength to take each day as it comes."

"We're all going to have to pitch in," I announced on Monday. By then I knew Loren would recover, but I didn't know when he would be back. I could only hope no one quit until that magic day.

No one quit, but it was close. "Ann, you're gyping us," Cindy announced as I conferred with a salesman. Backed by the other school girls, her voice stopped all conversation, and I felt my face redden.

"I'm paying all I can afford," I said, but I gave them each a little extra, wishing Loren were there. He'd have known what to do. And he'd have been better able to keep the men in the shop happy as they doubled up to do the extra work. The paper was my dream-come-true, but keeping it functioning often fell on my mate's shoulders, and I missed the comfort and security of having him to turn to. Ours was a Ma and Pa business, but I shuddered to think what would happen if something happened to Pa. Ma would panic.

If God was testing me to see if I really was capable of running the *News* alone, I was failing badly. It was a sobering thought to realize *my* answered prayer depended so heavily on my husband.

"Did you know the doctor's son is also a doctor?" Loren asked as I drove him home two weeks later. "He came in with his father—just wanted to look at my incision, I guess. He said his dad's way of treating the infection was different from his but he couldn't argue that it was working. Neither of them had any idea why peritonitis hadn't set in. They both think I'm pretty lucky to be here."

"We're all pretty lucky you're here," I said. "God has been good to us."

6

Our Paper

"They'll kill each other sometime," Loren muttered as he watched Sophie, Hattie, and Cora brake to stops from opposite directions. Each carried pages of news items, the type that had filled the paper for seventy-five years, the who-ate-dinner-where locals that are the bane of every weekly editor's existence. The younger generation snickers at them, but the older set can't seem to get enough. And with the help of these three, they got plenty, including the relationship of the diners to each other and the state of their health, such as "Mr. and Mrs. Charles Main were Sunday dinner guests of Mr. and Mrs. James Frane. Mrs. Main and Mrs. Frane are sisters. Mrs. Frane has been in poor health the past week, and Mrs. Main remained to care for her while Mr. Main returned alone." Reading them was difficult. Editing them was even worse. Every time I eliminated commas and relationships from Cora's copy, she fumed into the office, yelling, "God'll get you if you don't print it like I wrote it."

In spite of her threat to send God after us, we continued to edit her copy and she continued to bring it, if to do nothing more than to unearth more news than Sophie, who learned most of hers from her boarders and her daily walks around town.

We looked forward to the ladies' Monday visits as much as we cherished their times with us on Thursday afternoons. They showered us with love, fed us cookies and cake, and buoyed us up as we stared at less than perfect editions. If we had not been so caught up in deadlines, we would have realized it was something far more involved than their feelings for us that drew them to the offices—they loved the *News* and considered it their own.

Unfortunately, as with most of life's lessons, we did not realize this until we unconsciously violated their code of ethics for our paper.

"I can't stand to work in a shop that would print such an ad," Hattie Hooper snapped as she waved her copy of the *News* under our noses, pointing to an eight-inch advertisement for liquor. We hadn't wanted to publish it, but it was part of a contract we had inherited with our purchase of the *News* and we felt obligated to publish it.

"Would you call a daily paper to complain if it published an ad like that?" I asked.

"Oh, my no," she gasped. "I'd never do that to another paper. It's just that this one is, well, it's our paper."

Instead of being flattered that Hattie considered the *News* her paper, the community's paper, I was infuriated. It was *our* paper, Loren's and my paper, and it was the lifeblood of our family. Who was she to call it *her* paper?

By the end of the week, we learned Hattie wasn't the only person who considered the *News theirs.* Every church in town reported having prayed for us, for the removal of the offending advertisement from *their* paper.

"Being prayed for in church isn't the same as being excommunicated, is it?" we asked each other. We agreed it was not, but it was censure when we longed for encouragement.

"But we don't drink," we had told Silas Monroe when he warned we would become either alcoholics or religious fanatics, and it was still true. Yet liquor, much as we disliked it, coupled with our hurt pride, kept us from attending church.

It was a situation we could not have imagined in our wildest nightmares: my answered prayer to own the paper had severed our ties with church, with all churches, it seemed. It was an unhappy arrangement. We felt cast out and very alone, supported only by our faith in God. A prayer had been answered, but the cost would prove far dearer than we ever dreamed possible.

7

Do-It-Yourself Christianity

"We've come a long way since we were in high school and I ran the mimeograph and you slip sheeted, haven't we?" Loren asked as he watched me catch sheets as they came off the press and push them into place. Static, that constant bogeyman in print shops, was again creating havoc, and I was trying to prevent fires by keeping the printed pages in order.

"We sure have," I agreed. It was midnight. Our sons were home asleep and so, I imagined, was the baby sitter, trying to remember if this was the girl who rearranged furniture and dishes or the one who ate all the food in the house.

"Your rhythm is a whole lot better than it was then," he said.

"Thanks," I replied, sticking my tongue out at him. "It's just that I've added another motion."

"You're good at it, too. How do you hit that can so squarely? You should have blood all over the floor by now."

"Just luck, I guess," I grumbled as I caught a sheet and turned and spat into a large coffee can on the floor. I'd had a wisdom tooth extracted that day and the drainage showed no signs of stopping. But the lodge bulletin was due to be mailed the next day, and if the mailing crew was to have papers, it was up to Loren and me to supply them.

Schedules couldn't vary for wisdom teeth and, though they had altered somewhat for a ruptured appendix, they barely changed course when Doug was rushed to the hospital as convulsions wracked his body.

"Can't you help at all?" Loren asked, his eyes already gray from lack of sleep.

"I'll edit while he sleeps, but that's all for now. They expect me to be here with him."

"Why don't you let Alma stay with him? She sits with him every day anyway, so what difference does it make whether it's at home or in the hospital?"

"Because he's my son, not hers," I snapped peevishly, hating to admit I was scared of what people would say if I wasn't there with him: *Just a typical working mother.* I could hear the remarks and I didn't like the implication. It's one every working mother lives with, and it's a difficult obstacle to overcome.

Fortunately, drugs and medication broke Doug's raging fever, and he returned home two days later, too weak to crash through the house on his kiddy car or do anything except sleep. Leaving him with his devoted Alma, I took a shower and went back to work, every bone aching from having spent the nights trying to sleep in the contortionists' nightmare that passes for hospital visitors' chairs. I longed to yield to the temptation to take a nap, but it was Thursday, and I was needed. Always on Thursday.

Nor did a broken leg stay our Thursday deadline.

The leg belonged to Todd, a sturdy second grader. That golden September day my telephone rang, and Susan's frightened voice said, "Ann, be calm. There's been an accident and Todd's been hurt. Go to the hospital right away."

She hadn't said what had happened, but I decided he'd been hit by a ball bat. I calmly gathered together my purse and the work I'd planned to do at home after supper. A sweeping glance at my desk took in the pile of statements I'd just typed and I said aloud, "If he's in the hospital, we'll need money," as I scooped them up and carried them to the corner mail drop. And then I very calmly proceeded in six minutes to make a thirteen-mile trip down a state highway that wanders through a small town and twists past a river. Mario Andretti would have been proud of me.

Surprisingly, even though we had not yet learned that God creates calm in periods of great stress, we did not panic when the same patient country doctor who had calmed me when I knocked the top off my knee, who had delivered Doug, and who had helped save Loren's life determined the break in Todd's leg was too serious to be handled locally but would require treatment in a hospital fifty miles away. We even managed weak laughs as the nurse cut off Todd's blue jeans and our ever-modest son, his head swathed in bandages and still tender from the stitches necessary to close a huge cut, sat up and snarled, "All right! That's far enough!"

Like father, like son, I thought affectionately as I looked at two of my three redheads.

"Wonder how long he'll have to be at the hospital?" I asked Loren as we settled into the ambulance with Todd and began the long ride.

"Shouldn't be too long," he replied. "But don't worry about it. If they want a parent to stay, we can take turns. I'll stay the nights I don't have to run the press and you can stay while I print."

"We'll work out something," I said, remembering how disrupted our schedules had become when he and Doug had been ill. I wondered when Loren planned to sleep, but I praised God for His calming influence on both of us. He sustained us when we learned there would be no early dismissal for Todd, that he wouldn't be returning home or to the local hospital within the next few days but rather would remain in traction in the city hospital for at least six weeks.

"And they don't want parents staying over," we repeated to ourselves as we stopped for a midnight snack on the way home. It was hard to believe, and it came as a shock and with a sense of relief.

But even more surprising was the fact we were relaxing a little, enjoying each other's company. It had been years since we had gone out to eat. The food wasn't good, but we enjoyed it and each other. It was another of God's quiet miracles, and we rejoiced even in the face of a serious accident that had disrupted our lives. *God works in mysterious ways, His wonders to perform.* The words had never seemed more true.

And on Tuesday, we left right after lunch to visit our older son. Right after lunch on the day ads had to be prepared, copy rewritten. It was unthinkable, or it had been, but we did it. True, we returned to work well into the night, but we got almost as much done as if we'd worked straight through. And while we worked, we began to see an outpouring of love from the community that buoyed our spirits and reinforced our conviction that ours was a town that cared. People we scarcely knew sent gifts and cards. Family and friends visited Todd and played games with him during the long afternoons that preceded our evening visits. Norman P. Sandler came to the office every day to see how he was doing. "These little fellows mean a lot to us," he said, his voice cracking with emotion as he twirled his western style hat in his hand and shuffled from one expensive boot to the other.

Early autumn stretched into Indian summer and pre-winter, but we didn't miss a day of visiting our son. Alma and my parents alternated sitting with Doug, and on the nights neither of them could come, Hattie Hooper filled in, reading stories to Doug and spending the time after he went to bed cutting liquor ads from all our magazines. Patience Sandler, Vera Ross, and Sophie Palmer sent so many cookies and cakes we all gained weight.

We grew weary of the long trip, but we looked forward to seeing Todd and to the late snacks. We browsed in stores that stayed open after visiting hours, and the narrow confines of our existence moved back fifty miles. We shuddered to realize it had taken a broken leg to open up our world, to pull us out of our self-imposed shells.

"God certainly has been good to us," I said that crisp, cold pre-Thanksgiving day Todd returned home. "I wish we could do something to repay Him."

"There must be something," Loren replied.

We still felt cut off from church, but we valued our relationship with God. It was a sustaining influence in our lives, one we could not live without. We knew God doesn't expect repayment, that we can never repay Him for all He has done and continues to do for us, but we wanted to try. We sought new ways to serve Him while at the same time we had to come to grips with the realization that we could not do everything ourselves. We needed help as badly as we wanted to help. It was a confusing dilemma, and we prayed for a solution.

What we decided was the answer to both our problems was found in Loren's favorite section of a trade publication—the classified pages—where, under positions wanted, we found the name and address of a convict soon to be paroled. He wanted a job in a new community and a new chance at life.

God had given us so much, had so amply provided for our needs; there was nothing we wanted to do more than to share His bounty with others. Here was a man who wanted a new start. *I was in prison and you came to me.* The words from Matthew 25:36 became more vivid, more real, and we knew we wanted to help Bob even before we knew much about him.

"If you take this man and he doesn't work out, it won't prevent your trying again with another person, will it?" a parole officer asked.

"Oh, no," I replied enthusiastically. This was to be a repayment known only to God and ourselves. We saw no reason to tell anyone else. Still, the man needed a place to live, and the only honest thing to do was to explain the situation to prospective landlords or landladies.

"No," said Sophie Palmer when we approached her. I'd never heard her so emphatic about anything, and I was surprised. She frequently rented rooms, often for months or years at a time. But she would not rent to Bob. "It's too big a risk."

"The warden doesn't think he's dangerous," Loren assured her.

"What's he in for?"

"Parole violation."

"What'd he do?"

"Which time?"

"Either time. He had to do something to have a parole to violate."

But it was difficult to know where to begin in describing Bob's situation. Sent to a reformatory on a delinquency charge while still in his teens, he had been returned several times, always for parole violation, first for burglary, then for forgery. During his incarceration, he had learned the printing trade, an occupation he pursued following each of his releases. He had married and fathered a child, but the marriage had ended in divorce. Bitter and confused, he had been returned to the reformatory on yet another forgery charge.

Still, everyone who had worked with him had found him a good worker, and the social worker said he had no hesitation in recommending him if his parole was granted. That sounded good enough to us, and we made an offer he accepted.

Bob was coming to us through an inter-state compact agency via open heart surgery and a two-week recuperation. The recuperation went faster than the paperwork involved, and we chafed with impatience as time passed. If his social worker had no reservations about recommending him, we had absolutely none about hiring him. We'd get Bob here and worry about the details of his living arrangements later.

Bob was a good-looking man in his mid-twenties, slight of build with sandy hair and bright, blue eyes that never really looked directly at you when he was speaking but that sparkled with intelligence and humor. He could have been one of our own sons because of his build and coloring, but he had come to us from a background we would never understand, and his prison years had provided an education far different from the one he had cut short when he quit high school. His native humor and intelligence had been rechanneled by "educators" who would never taste freedom.

For the first two nights he bunked with Doug in the boys' bedroom, sleeping in Todd's bed since Todd, still encased in a heavy cast, was in the toy room downstairs. The room Bob and Doug shared joined ours, but, unlike Sophie, we were totally unafraid.

"Gee, this is just like home," Bob said as he joined us for meals and played with the boys, who soon came to regard him as a big brother.

But we couldn't expect a grown man to continue bunking with a baby, one prone to rattling his crib at 4 A.M. and given to amusing himself by rocking so hard the crib rolled into the other bed. And to move him into the toy room would rob the boys of a precious haven already invaded by a hospital bed. Clearly, Bob needed a place of his own.

"And his work is excellent," Loren added as he described Bob and his plight to Jed Benson, a man from our church who operated a mobile home court a stone's throw from the office.

"Then we should give him a chance," Jed replied.

Bolstered with a loan from his parents and a cash advance from us, Bob moved into his own home and we settled back into ours to herald his new life in rural America.

That was mistake number one.

Sheltered by family and friends, nurtured by two small communities, and kept busy in a world of newsprint, ink, and deadlines, we had never before encountered a person grown accustomed to institutionalization. We'd seen men in the army who could not have survived in civilian life, but we had never known anyone who had come to depend on an institution for everything.

"It wasn't too bad in the reformatory," Bob told us as we munched popcorn on one of his frequent visits to our home.

"They always got us up at the same time. The meals were good, and I liked the print shop. I knew what I was going to do at the same time every day."

"That's certainly different from our shop," Loren laughed.

"It's a nice shop, though," Bob said, "and I like the town. It's so quiet."

"It's a good town," I said. "There are wonderful people here. We don't go to church, but if you want to go, we'll take you."

"I don't go much, either," he said.

"We'll be glad to take you," Loren replied, but when Bob shook his head no we let the issue drop. We saw no reason to tell him about the misunderstanding that had separated us from our own church, nor did we insist he attend church.

That was mistake number two.

Bob's work was excellent. He could coax papers out of the press easily and was an apt student in the stereotype department.

"This is going to be a good deal for all of us," Loren said as we watched Bob set the old press into motion. Ever fearful Bob's still red scar would be damaged by too much lifting, Loren insisted on placing the forms on the press himself, but while Bob operated it he was free to work in the job department.

But we soon noted a change in our other employees. Susan, the bright-eyed optimist who had succeeded Peg and who always found good in everything and everyone, was tense and obviously upset about something.

"What's wrong?" I asked one day as I watched her eye Bob warily.

"Dad says if I get friendly with him, he'll make me quit," she said.

"He seems like a nice enough fellow. Your dad just doesn't know him."

"I know it, and that's what worries me. I'm scared of him."

"Who? Bob or your dad?"

"Bob. There's something funny about him. You don't see it as much as I do because you're at the other office most of the time.

But I work late some nights and when I do, I'm scared to death. He's okay when Loren's around, but he's different when Loren goes home for supper."

"Different?"

"Oh, you know, just different." She was on the verge of tears and obviously very frightened.

Tom wasn't frightened, and he was more direct. "Bob's not the same when you're not here," he said. "He's a wild man. Loren yells at the press, but Bob directs his obscenities at people. It's not the same."

"Has he threatened anyone?"

"He's threatened everyone in town."

"You and Susan and us?"

"No, none of us, but he's after everyone else. This town is too small for him. He's used to the city, and a town that rolls up its sidewalks every night at seven sharp isn't his cup of tea."

"Have you gone out with him?"

"We've been to the county seat for beer a couple of times. He gets a few drinks under his belt and he wants to fight everyone."

"He shouldn't drink with his heart condition," Loren said. "And he shouldn't fight. It hasn't been that long since his operation. He shouldn't even get agitated."

"Well, he's plenty agitated. He needs a woman."

"Maybe we can arrange a date with some nice girl," I said, already doing a mental inventory of every eligible female in town.

"I think Tom's saying he doesn't especially want a simple date," Loren said, interrupting my budding dating service.

"Sex?" I gasped. I had been sheltered, but I had read of men who thought only of the three-letter word we never printed. "Is that the reason Susan is afraid of him? Do you think he'd rape her?"

"Not really, but he can be pretty frightening after hours. He has two personalities. The one you see here is the good one. The other one is not Mr. Nice Guy trying to make good on the outside."

We didn't talk much over coffee and tea that night; instead, we stared mutely at each other, at a loss for words, and totally uncertain about what we should do next.

"Any time you have any problems you want to discuss, I'm willing to listen," Loren told Bob. Like me, he had no idea what to say. Our pressmen to date had included a sugarholic, a retired minister, a dedicated Christian family man, and a mechanical genius who had stayed long enough for Loren to have his appendix removed. Each had done his job with varying degrees of competence, much as Bob was doing his, and when each went home at night he was on his own. It had not occurred to us that a person who had spent the major portion of his adult years behind bars could not cope with twenty-four-hour-a-day freedom, especially with those hours between 5 P.M. and 8 A.M.

"I'm fine," Bob said.

"If there's anything I can't help you with, a really big problem, and you want to see the priest or go to church, Ann or I will take you until you get your own car," Loren said.

"It'll sure be good to get a car," Bob agreed, "but no, I don't need the church—and I sure don't need a priest."

Within days we were hearing rumbles that Bob had a girl friend. Not just any girl, but a fourteen-year-old, seven months pregnant, who could not name the father of her child. A fourteen-year-old willing to share her bed with Bob.

"What shall we do?" I asked Loren when Tom told us of Bob's romance, including details I wasn't positive I wanted to hear.

"What he does on his own time is his business," he replied. "Still, that girl's jail bait."

"She quit being jail bait about seven months ago," Tom said drily.

"But he should find a decent girl," I protested.

"That kind's not interested in him," Tom snorted. "You just don't know him."

Bob's work record was excellent. We said nothing, but we invited him home for supper more often. We couldn't keep him all night, but maybe we could keep some temptation away from him.

How naive we must have seemed to him. Sometimes he declined our invitations. Other times he came, but before we had left town on our trip home we'd see him going to the girl's apartment or leaving town with someone else.

And then he failed to report for work. Loren went in search of him and found his mobile home vacant. His girl friend did not know where he was, only that he had sold her father his television set just before he left. Further searching revealed he had used the money to buy a bus ticket, one way, as far east as he could go.

In two days he was back. "Boy, you should have seen the girl I sat with on the bus," he told Loren. "She had funny looking things on her hose and her skirt was real short."

"Bob, you've been a good worker. You've learned to do things no one else has liked to do and you haven't complained about it. But the reports we've been getting about your after-hours life aren't good. We still have parole reports to file, you know. We really want to help you. Let us take you to see the priest. I know him. He'll be glad to talk with you and help you work out your problems far better than I could."

"Got no problems, man," Bob replied. "Not after seeing that girl with the funny things on her legs."

It was almost Christmas, and we didn't want to ruin his first holiday spent in freedom by making him jobless. We let him return to work, and he moved back into the mobile home court.

"I would like to go home for Christmas," he said wistfully, and Loren agreed to take him to the bus station. But when he went to get him, Bob was already gone. He'd found another ride but had failed to tell Loren. Loren was irritated but still game. After all, Jesus had said the road would often be rough. The do-it-yourself road we were taking with Bob was bound to be even more difficult.

Bob returned after the holidays, and for two weeks it appeared everything was going well with our new printer. Then he was gone again, this time for four days. "I'll stay until you can find a replacement," he offered when he came into the shop late at night where Loren was again burning midnight oil.

"It's no use, Bob," Loren said. "You just can't take small town life. You should go back to the city."

"You mean I'm fired?" Bob asked.

"I'm afraid so," Loren said sadly.

"That's okay. Don't worry about it, man. I'll see you later."

"Want a ride to the bus?"

"Sure."

"How about the stuff in your trailer?"

"Leave it there. I'll get it later."

Wondering when "later" might be for a man leaving the community for good and worried at our failure with Bob, Loren noticed Tom's car headed in the opposite direction as he returned from the county seat where he had deposited Bob at the bus station, but he thought little of it. They waved and went on their separate ways.

"Had to go get Bob from the bus station last night," Tom reported the next morning.

"What do you mean, you had to *get* him? I just took him there," Loren said.

"Said he'd just gotten there and he wanted to see his girl friend, so I took him to her place."

"He must've called you as soon as I let him off," Loren said.

"Probably why we passed each other."

A week later, Bob called Loren from the bus station and asked him to call his mother. By then we knew he'd left his mobile home with the pipes frozen and the drain out of commission. Several bars were looking for him to collect past due accounts.

Loren called Bob's mother and as kindly as he knew how, told her about Bob's latest escapades. She wasn't surprised, only heartbroken that he couldn't shake the pattern.

"I want to help," Loren said.

"There's nothing you can do."

"There must be something," Loren said. Together we called the priest. Bob wouldn't go see him, but perhaps the priest could give us suggestions that would help.

Again we were disappointed. "I was a prison chaplain for five years. I know the kind of man you're talking about. There's nothing you can do to help him. He's used to being in an institution, and he's doing everything he can to get back there. He's following a pattern only he can break."

A call to Silas Monroe was equally unrewarding. "I've seen your man. He doesn't want to be helped. And he can't or won't help himself."

Finally, Bob's parole officer advised him to stay in Indiana and get work, and Bob promised to look.

"I found a good job in a print shop," he told us the last day we saw him, and we prayed he would stick with it.

But he didn't have a job, and he drifted for weeks that were broken for us by tearful telephone calls from his mother. "He's following a pattern," she said, her words echoing those of Silas Monroe and the priest. "Whenever something goes wrong, he blows up and leaves. He didn't leave because of you or the job but because his drain quit working. He can't cope with everyday life."

Bob came back to town several times after that, but we never saw him again. But Tom and the bars did. "Loan me a hundred dollars," he demanded as he drove up to Tom's house in a new Cadillac.

"Don't have that much money," Tom replied.

"How about fifty?"

"No."

"Five?"

"No."

"Enough for a six-pack?"

"No."

"How about a nickel?"

"Here you go," Tom said as he flipped the coin to him and

watched Bob wheel the big car around and head back to the bar.

We didn't see him, but we heard from him often. He wrote from another town that he had a job. But that was short-lived, he told me when he called to report he was back home. "The city's the place for me," he said, and I prayed he was right.

For the next two or three years, I received occasional calls from Bob, the friendliest, most likeable flop at do-it-yourself Christianity we ever undertook. He was back in jail a number of times, but, finally, inevitably, he wrote from the reformatory again. He'd been in a fight and he'd fled to another state, forging a series of checks enroute. But he was happy; extradition had included a flight across four states. "It was my first plane ride," he boasted in his letter. He was back in his favorite reformatory, the one that let him work in the print shop, and he was satisfied. Every line of his letter said he had come home.

Bob was happy, but we were left with a sense of failure, both at our attempts to help him and with our do-it-yourself Christianity. What, we kept asking ourselves, could be done to help a person like Bob? Where had we gone wrong? Where had he gone wrong? Would psychiatric care have helped? Where had his parents failed? Had society failed? What was the answer for people like him?

We were left fumbling for answers. All we could do was thank God it had not been necessary for the police to take Bob at his word when he told us, "They'll have to shoot me to get me back," or that he had not shot someone else after "blowing up."

His uncontrollable high and low periods gave us cause to reflect on our own situation. That could have been why God sent him to us. At the time, however, all we could do was pray that God would forgive us for allowing our faith to waiver because our works had failed.

Ephesians warns: "For by grace you have been saved through faith; and this is not your own doing, it is the gift of God—not because of works, lest any man should boast."

But we were not boasting. Bob's was one story that never saw print in the *News*. It was a story of failure, and we prided our-selves on reporting successes. "The Bible Belt Blabber," Cora termed the *News*. "Always concentrating on the good and giving the churches too much space."

"We want good news," readers said when they called to com-plain about our reporting their sons' arrests. "Leave the bad news to the city papers." But they flocked to the newsstands to buy every copy of daily papers that had blood-dripping murder pic-tures on page one, and when a tornado leveled our area, they not only bought every copy of the *News* but some demanded we order a reprint.

Herbert Bayard Swope, one of New York City's most famous reporters, once gave his formula for failure: "Try to please every-body."

But we did not report a word about Bob, neither his coming nor his going. We were not really trying to please everyone—just God and ourselves—and we'd failed miserably.

8

God Doesn't Like Quitters

The world Bob had brought to our door was one that we knew existed, but our previous exposure had been vicarious at best. We had never known anyone like him. Our sense of failure was an unwieldy burden.

"What are we going to do?" Loren asked as we drank tea and coffee. We had to have help, but where would it come from? Certainly not from Tom. He was working as hard as he could. Susan was doing all she could. Loren and I were both stretched too far now. It had to come from outside. Paul Carter offered his assitance, but we declined, feeling he was more needed at home than in our shop, but we rejoiced he still cared enough to offer. Our estrangement from church and our failure with Bob seemed to widen the gulf between us and the world, one we longed to bridge but didn't know where to begin. Paul's offer to help was far more welcome than he'll ever know.

Loren stared into his coffee cup and murmured, "We've got to figure out a way to get some help or else get rid of the lodge bulletin."

"So do it," I said. "I'm tired of your being gone every night. I'm fed up with having so many bills for newsprint."

"It'll never work," he said. But by the time he came home the next evening, his frown had given way to a smile. Faced with a stack of unpaid bills and the prospect of another deadline for the monthly paper, he had reassessed the publication and called

Orlando to tell him it might be best if he found a new printer.

"Was he angry?" I asked, remembering my first meeting with the tall man I'd come to respect but who might still be capable of becoming as infuriated as he had been when I rejected his poem.

"I don't know. I didn't ask him." And with that my weary mate sank into his recliner, tilted back, and went sound asleep while I wondered how we would make the payments if we really did quit publishing the monthly paper.

Orlando and Lloyd stopped by the office the next day. Orlando, again elegant in his faded Sunday best, his hair a frosty cap of silver, spoke first. "We just wanted to come and thank you for all you've done for us."

"I hope you aren't angry," I said hesitatingly.

"Shucks no," Lloyd replied, slapping Loren on the back, his short arms barely reaching my husband's shoulders. "This is a good guy you married, Ann, but he can't carry the weight of the world himself, much less put all his faith in that crazy press of yours. Besides that, Orlando and I've been thinking of moving south, maybe get a little warmth into these old bones."

Within a few days the brothers had moved out their mailing equipment, fitting it into Lloyd's van for the trip south. "We just decided to take it with us," Lloyd said. "We've had so much experience putting out a newspaper here that we feel we can help the next printer."

"May God have mercy on his soul," Loren said, but he was smiling a happy smile that brightened his blue eyes and erased the lines of fatigue.

"Do you think Cora and Nettie and Vera will ever come see us again?" Todd asked sadly as we watched the widows leave the mailing room for the last time. "They sure made good cookies."

"Don't worry about snacks," Loren assured him. "Your mother will still be making popcorn."

"Someone has to," I said, grinning broadly. God certainly had His ways of returning things to normal.

The extra Linotype was sold, and some of the bills paid with the proceeds. We found that the publication we had thought would help pay other expenses had actually plunged us deeper into the red. The weekly newspaper we had published for the out-of-town editor had folded, and we found ourselves back to two. Two papers. Two sons. The prospect seemed as bright as it had the day Doug was born, and it offered us more time to do what we wanted to do. Loren would be freer to pursue job work while I concentrated on the two weeklies. We would have more time to spend with the boys.

It should have been a time for celebration. Instead, it became a time for reevaluation, a time of disillusionment. Cast loose from church ties, we had attempted do-it-yourself Christianity and in the process had seen a man swept away by forces he couldn't seem to control. We'd told the parole officer we wouldn't be afraid to try again with another man, but the truth was that we felt unable to control the forces that surrounded us and *were* afraid to try again.

We decided to sell the papers, to rid ourselves of the albatross that hung heavily on Loren, that created mixed emotions within us.

"What have you always wanted to do?" Loren asked.

"Write."

"You're doing that. What else?"

"Own the *News*," I replied glumly. I needed no more reminders that my prayers had been answered, but he was not in a reminding mood. "Besides that?"

"Finish college, I guess."

"So, go." It was an order, and I suddenly found myself back in the world of textbooks and term papers. There was neither time nor money to be a full-time student, but we sold some corn, and I salvaged enough money to pay for evening classes. Fifteen years after I abandoned my dreams of a journalism degree to get married, I was back in school to get a degree in languages, primarily because the small, church-related college to which I'd transferred my university credits did not offer journalism. Besides, I reasoned, I was getting enough on-the-job training to last a lifetime.

The college required each student to take three courses in religion in order to graduate, and I found myself up to my ears in an academic search for the historic Jesus, discussions of existentialism, a theory I'd never heard of before, and the study of the works of a number of renowned theologians. It was stiff reading for a person weaned on Nancy Drew, whose knowledge of the Bible barely extended past the Golden Rule and the Ten Commandments, and who hadn't been inside a church for years.

In the meantime, we used other farm income for Loren to fulfill his lifetime dream of learning to fly. Selling the papers would mean new directions for both of us, and we were ready and willing to be prepared. Meals became times of lively discussions with the boys describing their daily lives, Todd at school and Doug at home with Alma. To this was added a strange new world of flying the omni, headings, points and turns, magnetos, and touch and go that was mixed with timid explorations of existentialism, the lives of Rudolph Bultmann and Soren Kierkegaard.

"Don't you ever just study the Bible?" Todd asked.

"We just read about people who study it."

"That sounds like a waste of time."

Loren was more direct. "If you won't talk about religion anymore, I won't talk about flying."

"Fair enough," I said, although I longed to discuss the theories my teenaged classmates seemed to accept without question.

"My religious philosophy is pretty liberal," I wrote on a term paper, "but like Bultmann's, it tends to swing. I once was a Sunday school teacher and an active church worker. The pendulum may swing in that direction again and when it does, I may have a more fundamental outlook."

"You might, but I doubt it," the professor wrote across the paper.

Confused by my religion courses, I found it easy to drop out of school again the night I came home from work and the boys said in unison, "Hi, Mom. Who's going to sit with us tonight?"

They meant no harm in their casual question, but it was a sore reminder that I neglected them in favor of college, clubs, and work. Work had to continue but the others did not. I dropped my classes and resigned from all the clubs to which I belonged, a move that wasn't very difficult when I realized how very little I contributed to any of the organizations.

Loren's flying lessons continued, however, and for the first time in years we found ourselves doing something together, all of us. We flew to visit my brother in Michigan, to get Linotype parts in Ohio, to an air show in Wisconsin. Our world enlarged, and we enjoyed ourselves so much that we didn't panic when the *News* did not sell.

I remembered a sign Hattie Hooper used to keep in our Sunday school classroom: *God doesn't like quitters.* It was apparent He didn't want us to be quitters, and we wanted to do His will. Without Him we could never have published one issue. With Him, we could cheerfully say, "Always on Thursday," and we would continue to use that as our slogan even as we both knew we had changed from the day we adopted the motto. We were not the same happy-go-lucky couple we had been before answered prayer became a reality, but we weren't quitters, either.

9

Twins in One Skin

For six years we nursed Doug through sickness and health, watching him evolve from a tiny, red-faced baby into a bundle of energy who awoke hours before the rest of the family, mixed dry coffee, sugar, and flour together for the fun of it, and seemed to go out of his way to tease. Mischief glinted in his brown eyes, and people meeting him for the first time invariably whispered, "Boy, I'll bet he's a handful." We could only nod agreement; keeping up with Doug was a full-time job, one that involved a sitter's care every day as well as the care Loren and I gave him.

Twice as stubborn, twice as temperamental, twice as dirty, twice as persistent as one boy should be, he carried home enough junk for two, keeping us so busy clearing Linotype mats, bicycle chains, knotted string, and dead snakes out of his room that we didn't have time to analyze his behavior. Besides, he could be twice as loving as most six-year-olds, and we relished those times together.

We only laughed when a doctor told us Doug had an extra bone in his foot and when a trip to an oral surgeon was needed to remove an extra tooth, a "supernumerary." "We had twins in one skin," we joked.

And so it seemed. No one boy could do all the things he did. By the time he started kindergarten his list of pranks was long, not unlike many five-year-olds, but active to say the least.

But these events were few and far between when considered over his lifetime, and we attributed them in part to his being more than a little spoiled by parents, grandparents, Todd, and his ever-devoted Alma. Temperamental, but loving and lovable, our little red-head was a captivating guy, and we tried to accentuate the positive and eliminate the negative as much as possible.

Doug entered kindergarten with zest, coming home the first day to announce solemnly, "Well, some girl has me for a boy friend." Five years old and in love with a stranger. He was off to a good start!

He entered first grade with enthusiasm, preferring recess to all other subjects, but we weren't overly concerned because Todd had been a reluctant scholar who exasperated teachers by staring out the windows but always responded with the right answers if called on. He'd had private speech therapy and enough remedial reading that he had soon read far above his grade level. He'd made excellent grades when he tried; it might just take Doug a bit longer to want to make the effort. But by mid-year we knew the truth of the statement that no two children are alike. Something far more serious was the matter. Doug's I.Q. was very high, his grades so low it appeared that he might fail.

Loren and I groped for ways to help Doug, to make his homework easier, less boring, and less frustrating for all of us. We prayed for the added strength it would take to cope with our six-year-old, aching to help him, uncertain when we would find the extra time he needed, and what the answer to the problem might be.

The voice of God is often a still, small voice, and the answer we received to our anguished cries for help was unrecognized as such, but now we count our blessings that Doug awoke one day with his face swollen round as a full moon. There would be no school that week for our reluctant scholar, and he was bound to fall further behind.

"Best case of mumps I've seen for a while," our doctor said when he examined Doug.

If Doug had not had mumps we would not have seen a doctor

and I never would have blurted out the question that was dancing through my mind. "Is there any reason Doug is failing first grade when he has a high I.Q.?"

Instead of laughing and telling me that Doug was a lazy student who hadn't yet decided to work, he replied gravely, "Yes, there is." He sent Doug into another room and explained. "Doug is hyperkinetic."

"Hyper what?"

"He's hyperkinetic. His brain works faster than his body can keep up."

Immediately, I was ready to take the blame. I'd heard of hyperkinesis, but I knew little about it except it sounded bad, and I was certain our schedules and my bad temper had caused it.

"I fell down a couple of times while I was pregnant with him," I remembered. "And his cord was knotted so tightly the doctor said if it had been any tighter he would have died." I didn't wait for the doctor to say anything as I recalled, "And he used to get sick without any warning. Nothing we could do seemed to keep his temperature down, and one time he went into convulsions and had to be hospitalized."

When I finally paused for breath, the doctor said, "If you'll slow down a minute, I want to tell you something very important."

I waited.

"Nothing you did or did not do caused it."

The relief I felt was overwhelming, except I still hadn't confessed to having my sugar count get too high while I was pregnant or to being upset as I made maternity clothes while I watched John F. Kennedy's televised funeral. Or all the other events that had added stress to what was otherwise an uneventful pregnancy.

The doctor reached into his file and pulled out a sheet of paper containing the symptoms of hyperkinesis. "Any of these traits sound familiar?"

I read:

1. *Abnormal motor activity.* The child is overactive, fidgets, jumping from one activity to another, talking in disorganized torrents.

2. *Poor coordination.* Often clumsy, the child has trouble making his eyes and hands work together.

3. *Impulsiveness.* A hyperkinetic child can't seem to keep from touching everything and everyone. He acts and talks before he thinks, is unpredictable and often unmanageable.

4. *Short attention span.* He has difficulty concentrating on any one thing, such as what the teacher is saying or what is written on the blackboard. He's easily distracted.

5. *Perceptual disabilities.* The child does not see what others see or hear what they hear although there is nothing wrong with his eyes, ears or other sense organs.

6. *Specific learning problems.* Reading, writing, spelling, and arithmetic often are difficult for the child, but he may do very well in some areas, poorly in others. His over-all I.Q. score may be in the average or above range but he will score quite high on some sub tests and very low on others.

7. *Emotionally highstrung.* Often irritable, overly sensitive, quick tempered, explosive, moody, hard to live with, flashing between temper tantrums and remorse. He panics easily and his tolerance for failure and frustration is low.

8. *Language disorders.* Speech irregularities are common; he may be slow to talk and hard to understand.

"They all sound familiar," I said when I'd finished reading the list. "Doug's always been on the move. He's gotten into more things than any other boy I know. He's not always clumsy, but he had a hard time learning to tie his shoes. And he's never been able to keep his hands to himself. The teacher says he can't concentrate and seems to be having problems with all his subjects, especially reading. And you'd better believe he's temperamental, but we always figured he inherited that trait. He was slow learning to talk. After all, when you have a lot of devoted people willing to do anything for you, what's the sense of learning to talk? We've taken him to audiologists and ophthalmologists, but they couldn't find anything wrong with his hearing or vision."

"Any child can have some of those problems, but not all of them," the doctor said. "I've been watching Doug for a long time, and he seems to be a classic hyperkinetic."

"If you've been watching him, why didn't you say something?" I asked. We liked this man to whom we turned when our faithful country doctor died. He and Loren were friends who belonged to the same club, and Doug had frequently accompanied his father to the meetings. The doctor had had more time to observe Doug's behavior than most doctors have to see their patients.

"You didn't ask me. Parents have to be ready to acknowledge a problem exists before a doctor can help," he said.

I wasn't certain I agreed with his philosophy, but I knew it was time to do something. "Where do we go from here?" I asked, totally unprepared for his answer.

"Right now, putting him on medication is the only solution," he said.

"Drugs?"

"Yes. An amphetamine. It would have you or me climbing the walls, but Doug's brain is working faster than it can send signals to his body, and the medication will equalize the two. He should be quieter, better able to concentrate."

"Could I talk to Loren about this before we do anything?" I asked. This was more than I wanted to undertake without getting my husband's opinion.

The doctor agreed and gave me a handful of information to study and a cassette for us to listen to.

I took Doug home and settled him in the living room with a book, hoping he'd stay there long enough for me to call Loren and tell him the news.

"Wow," he said after I'd repeated the doctor's words.

His choice of expletives was appropriate. "Wow," we said after we'd read the brochures and listened to the tape. Ours was not going to be an easy role even if Doug did use the drug. "He needs help," one booklet said, "from the doctor, the school, and especially from you."

"*Especially from you.*" The words bore into our hearts, and we knew we would do what we could. If only there could be more hours in the day, more days in the week. But this was not possible, and we would have to do what we could with our own limited time resources.

After two weeks of prayer and uncertainty in which Doug recovered from the mumps and returned to school for two days before developing the best case of chicken pox the doctor had ever seen, we decided to try the medication. We were encouraged that most specialists agreed there was little likelihood the child would later develop a dependence on drugs.

But there could be minor to severe side effects, we were told, and we watched for loss of appetite, weight loss, insomnia, depression, headaches, stomach aches, bed wetting, irritability, and dizziness. Instead, we found a boy with a still ravenous appetite who slept better than ever, who was easier to get along with, who could sit still without constantly jumping up and down. In short, our bundle of joy was a joy to behold—when he took his medicine. We could control the morning pill but we had to depend on him to take the little white tablet at noon. Before long, we were able to tell within thirty seconds or less if he had taken the noon pill simply by listening to him when he came home from school. If he had not taken it, he was higher than the proverbial kite, highstrung, and easily upset. If he had taken it, he was calm and relaxed.

"Why do you forget your pill?" we asked, and he always shrugged his shoulders and muttered that he'd forgotten, but we sensed there was more to it than that. Finally, he sobbed, "The other kids make fun of me. I'm the only person in my class who has to take a pill."

The doctor remedied the situation by changing the dosage,

and we were able to go on to the rest of Doug's treatment, because the drug was not all of it. There would be therapy, and that was where Loren, Todd, and I were to help. Our goal was to enable Doug to feel less frustration. "He needs gratification in order to help his emotional development and to enable him to receive the greatest possible benefits from the education available during this period," we were told.

And we were also told to exercise more control over ourselves in relation to Doug. In short, no nagging but punishment if necessary, such as taking away privileges instead of spanking. "Don't threaten disciplinary action unless you can immediately execute it," we were cautioned. We found effective results came from depriving him of his favorite television program or withholding dessert. He resented it, but it worked, even if we did feel villainous.

And there must be routine. We hadn't known regular hours since we bought the paper years before Doug was born, but we said we'd try. Meal times had to be at the same time every day, and, to our surprise, we found they not only could be but that the regularity was a blessing for all of us—no longer would Loren come home and wait for supper; no longer would I try to keep his supper hot. We all ate at the same time every day.

There were to be no surprises. "Our very way of life is a surprise," I protested to the doctor. "We never know when the phone will summon us to a fire or a train derailment. We take the boys along when we take pictures. It makes them feel a part of our lives and lets them have the experience of seeing the event firsthand."

"Everyone's life is full of surprises," he admonished. "Just make certain yours does not have too many."

I reflected on his advice and realized we'd seldom told the boys in advance that we were going to Grandma's house or that friends were coming. They always asked so many questions it seemed simpler to surprise them than to have them ask, "When are we going?" "How long is it yet?" We came to understand those questions were part of the reassurance our children, especially our six-year-old, needed, and we tried to answer them without becoming impatient, even when they were asked ten or fifteen times. We finally understood that refusing to share our plans with Todd and Doug was in effect breaking the Golden Rule. I don't want to be greeted with three extra supper guests on a night I've baked four pot pies anymore than Loren wants to have a party after he's worked three days and nights end-running. Sharing our plans with the boys created more questions, but it resulted in less apprehension, less uncertainty, and it told them that they, and their own plans, counted.

We were advised to give Doug a separate room of his own, so the toy room gave way to a bedroom where he could work on homework or be sent if his behavior didn't conform.

The doctor had done his part by prescribing and supervising the medication; we were doing ours by helping establish guidelines. But what about that third member of the important group that had to help our son—his school? We explained the problem to his teacher and described the medication. She was pleased we had done something to quiet him, but she was frightened by the possible side effects of the drug. In her mind, she marked him as a "very special child" and avoided giving him more than minimal attention.

The fault wasn't all hers. With a room full of normally active first graders, she was unable to do much. We continued working with Doug, helping mostly with reading since that was the area in which his greatest difficulty lay. But we were not trained teachers; we were parents who also worked, who came home exhausted, made even more weary by the prospects of facing another battle with our son.

A noted allergist has estimated four million children in the United States share Doug's problem, four out of every one hundred grade school children. Most classroom teachers, however, are ill-prepared to cope with the strange affliction that affects boys more often than girls and seldom more than one child in a family. Administrators tend to classify the children as under-motivated, slow maturing, or just plain lazy.

Our school system, amply staffed and equipped for sports, offered little in the way of remedial education. There was nothing for children as young as Doug. Geared for the average child, it offered little for gifted children, those who should be in special education classes, or the hyperkinetics who fit neither category.

The administration showed considerable lack of enthusiasm for any of these programs. School board members accustomed for years to seeing me quietly taking notes suddenly found me staying after meetings to protest a system that offered so little for children with learning disabilities. "If we can afford all that sports equipment, why can't we have special reading programs or speech therapy?" I asked.

"But, Ann, we have facilities for swimming, wrestling, track, football, basketball, and gymnastics and we have to use them," administrators said. "We have to expand in that area." One was even heard to mutter, "Gee, I suppose next they'll want us to buy braces for their kids' teeth if they need them."

"Do you want a generation of athletes who can't read?" I sputtered, hating myself for being dangerously close to tear level. I prayed God would forgive my anger, but I knew, too, the concern he felt for *His* son, for *all* our sons. I remembered the anger and impatience Jesus showed with the money changers in the temple when He could no longer stand their deceit, and I wished I had a fraction of His courage.

My own battle coincided with one led by a group of concerned mothers who also demanded help for their children, the dyslexics who had difficulty learning to read, write, and spell because they tended to confuse the letters b and d, p and q. Or, as one boy put it, "I just can't remember which side of the circle to put the stick on." Doug also fit into this group, and I could sympathize with the mothers' plight as they attempted to help their sons. Like hyperkinesis, the affliction strikes boys far more often than girls. The causes are not entirely understood, but they seem to fall into three separate categories: pre-natal, during birth, and after birth. During birth, too little oxygen to the brain can be a factor, and after birth, a high fever can often trigger it. Doug fit two out of three categories. To have named him in print, however, would have been a violation of our mother-son relationship and would have smacked of partisan journalism. But I could go to bat for the other mothers, the other sons, and I did.

The articles and editorials won awards, and the parents were pleased with the support, but nothing was done for those precious children we wanted to have the same opportunities as those without perceptual difficulties. We drew comfort from the list of dyslexics who had succeeded in the world: Albert Einstein, Thomas Edison, Auguste Rodin, Hans Christian Anderson, George Patton, Nelson Rockefeller. Obviously, these men's lives disputed the administration's implied suggestion that we asked too much when we pleaded for more individualized education for our sons, too much because they were "probably retarded anyway." They were not retarded, but in a school system geared for the average, they often were left out. It fell to us as concerned parents to offer tutoring we were ill equipped to provide and patience we often lacked when it was sorely needed.

Frustrated at the lack of support we received from the school system, we plodded along, remaining silent about Doug's problem, convinced that somehow, some way, we would conquer it, praying to be tougher than it was. Progress was slow, often painful, but as the years went by, we began to see changes, an evolution that began with a never-ending tree house described in *Born Again . . . but still wet behind the ears.* Pictures of Doug working on the sturdy structure that never rose higher than an old elm stump show a pudgy, very dedicated craftsman, one whose hands and mind were obviously working together. The sound of his steady work was music to our ears, an answered prayer, the culmination of hours of help from Alma, from Sophie Palmer, from his grandparents, and from us, his parents, those imperfect pieces of clay from which God was trying to mold something useful and productive.

The sound of Doug's hammering was beautiful, almost as glorious as the doctor's eventual decision that Doug could discontinue the drug.

He'd originally told us the medication would be discontinued before Doug reached puberty, that it would be less needed then because his body chemistry would be leveling out. "But he just doesn't need it any longer," he told us the summer of the tree house.

We were greatly relieved. No more struggles to get him to take his medicine, no more worrying about over-dosage. But we were also worried we wouldn't be able to control him without drugs. However, we noticed little difference, and our lives settled into a new orderliness that was as unorderly as before, because we were in no way finished with Doug's therapy.

The tree house alone was not the answer, anymore than was the restructuring of our lives, the tutoring, the patience we had to muster—and this was crucial because living with a hyperkinetic child is not easy; it's difficult not to become frustrated and angry.

Prayer helped lighten our cross, but we shut off another avenue that would have been highly beneficial, too—simply talking about our problem. We drew strength from God, but if we had let ourselves talk about the problem sooner, we would have learned we were not really alone in our battle, that even in our rural area there were others who had hyperkinetic sons, as well as parents of dyslexics. Not as many as the statistics indicate there should be, but they were there, those parents who also worried and prayed. We would have learned we were not the only parents who lost our tempers—this was normal and to be expected. We would have drawn some comfort (maybe a perverse comfort) from knowing our child was able to cope on ten milligrams of the drug while others were still highly hyperactive on sixty.

Without the drug, a method of treatment now being questioned by doctors, we searched for new ways to help our son, knowing he still faced problems that could result in his developing failure syndromes that could lead to his becoming a drop-out, getting into trouble, or developing a negative lifestyle or delinquent behavior.

Allergists have done a lot of research into the cause of this problem, reaching the conclusion that part of its wildfire spread can be blamed on food additives, artificial coloring, and sweeteners. Others blame fluorescent lights, milk drinking, low-level lead poisoning, oxygen deprivation at birth (which in Doug's case could have been a contributing factor), but no one has positively determined what causes hyperkinetic children, those one doctor compares to a revved up motor with the throttle stuck.

Loren and I aren't doctors any more than we are teachers. We can't say conclusively that taking away Doug's taco chips and cola drinks was the answer, only that it helped. We do know that giving him a cup of coffee often had the same effect his pills used to produce, but it was a treatment we resorted to only when all other attempts to calm him failed.

Speech therapy, remedial reading, even summer school for students with learning problems, were finally introduced into our school system and were meticulously reported to our readers. Doug was able to participate in some of the programs, although he hated them every bit as much as the administration predicted he would.

The treehouse that seemed to mark a turning point for Doug no longer exists. It was his treasured refuge until he dismantled it, taking boards from it to use in a building that in no way resembles its haphazard predecessor. It is a small, very complete workshop in which our budding craftsman can work happily, his hands in perfect harmony with his busy brain.

We look to Doug's future with a renewed thanks to Him who was a carpenter—and of whose teen years the Bible is silent—praying for wisdom to commit our sons and ourselves into His care each day. We thank the Carpenter, in whose hands we place our lives, that Doug is finally to the point his tests long ago indicated—the point of being able to live up to his capabilities. What more could any man desire?

10

Turning Points

God heard prayers of thanksgiving throughout the week, always on Thursday, and sometimes at midnight when the days stretched into each other. And He heard prayers of supplication: for strength, courage, and stamina.

But in spite of my prayer life, something was lacking, and it seemed the answer might lie in my severed church relations. After all, we were the ones who made the break. The church had done nothing to us. We often prayed for other people, yet we were denying them the same right by being offended when they in turn prayed for us.

I swallowed my pride and attended several services, but the old hurt wouldn't die, it wouldn't be surrendered. I sat hunched in the pew, clutching it tightly, letting it eat into my system while all the while I longed to let go of it, to feel what others evidently did the Sunday a team of visiting lay persons spoke. Several went forward and recommitted their lives to God. I remained in my pew, immobile, afraid of what people would think or say.

And the hurt stayed with me. Even the hot tears I shed, tears of frustration at my own lack and tears of joy for those who were surrendering their lives to God, didn't wash away the hurt. Instead I wept all the harder, for myself, for Loren, for what seemed like a shattered answer to a prayer and for something so close, yet so far. It wasn't surprising that I soon found it simpler to stay home. Until I could take my problems to God, surrender them and leave them in His care without tugging them back with me,

I would be better off taking rides with my family or even staying home while they sought their own diversions.

But I was not alone.

For years we had felt the presence of a ghost in our house, a friendly spirit mostly given to moving up and down stairs rather noisily and to opening doors very quietly. If the ghost had not also been prone to stealing scissors and doing such bizarre things as leaving bundles of hair on the living room floor—red and straight like Loren's and brown and curly like mine—we would have paid little attention to him. But finding bundles of hair neatly tied with black thread is unnerving, and we paid more than a little attention to the invisible poltergeist that also delighted in leaving the hall light on until we went to investigate, only to find the hall dark—and empty. He moved tin cans around the attic at will, old, rusty cans with faded labels outdated before we were born.

We first felt the ghost's presence shortly after we moved to the old house that now has been home for so many years. We sensed the poltergeist was a man who once lived there but later disappeared very mysteriously. To this day, no one knows if he is dead or alive, but for too long something we determined was his spirit invaded our house, coming and going at will. Nothing else he did was as frightening as the hair and scissor episodes, and we soon accepted "him" as a part of our lives, wishing only he could be neater with those old cans and that his presence didn't frighten Doug so badly.

"What is that noise on the stairs?" Alma demanded one night when I returned from the office. "It sounds like someone walking up and down the steps, but there's never anyone there."

"I don't know," I said. "We think it's a ghost."

To my surprise, she wasn't the least bit startled. "Who is he?" she whispered.

I told her.

"Oh, him!" she snorted. "Don't worry about him. I always did wonder what happened to that guy, but I sure wouldn't be scared if I saw him. It'd be kind of fun to talk to him."

If Alma did not object to sharing the house with the ghost, we saw no reason to do anything about removing him. The sound of his movements became as familiar as our own as he wandered endlessly up and down the stairs.

The ghost stayed with us until a rare, long weekend I should have used to clean but instead spent scrunched in a chair reading a book so full of suspense I became oblivious to everything around me. The moor country of England provided the eerie setting in which the heroine was met at every turn by veiled threats of death. The house had eyes, all of which seemed to focus on her. Each page became more gripping, and as I read, I heard the footsteps come down my own stairs and saw the door open, but I didn't pay any attention to the motion. The sounds were reassuring, warm and friendly compared with the watching eyes of the old house in which the heroine tried to find comfort and love.

I read frantically, ignoring the strange sounds in our own old house. I was within twenty pages of the end of the book, the outcome still a mystery, when the telephone rang and Todd asked permission to stay longer at a friend's house. "Please do," I said nervously, eager to return to the book. The sound woke Doug, a sturdy toddler more frightened by the ghost than any of us. He joined me in my chair until he, too, heard the footsteps and fled to the kitchen to seek a snack.

At last, the mystery was solved, the person I had suspected was indeed haunting the old house and the young people lived happily ever after.

It was only then I realized how late it was, that Todd had come home and joined Doug at the refrigerator. I rushed to the kitchen, rescued what food was left, and called the family to supper where I described the book I'd read.

"Sounds wild," Loren said.

"It was," I agreed. "It makes our ghost seem like a pipsqueak. He couldn't begin to keep up with the things that happened in that old house."

"He is sort of namby-pamby most of the time," Loren agreed, and Todd said that according to books he'd read, our ghost was a sissy.

We all laughed uproariously, refreshed by a day at home, but totally unprepared for what happened next.

The footsteps, which never before had left the stairway, were heard descending, rapidly. They continued into the living room, through the dining room and into the kitchen. We all watched, unbelieving, as the knob turned, the door opened and then slammed shut.

The ghost has never returned. Our laughter removed him forever, and, after our initial surprise, we rejoiced that he was gone. "A demon spirit," a friend told us later. We knew nothing of demons, only that there is evil loose in the world and maybe a bit of it had come to live with us. Our immediate feeling was one of relief that the disappearance quieted some of Doug's fears, even if it did sometimes seem a little dull without footsteps, opening doors, and cans. But we knew it was for the best.

It was a time we should have rejoiced and told our story to others, but we did not. Nor did we know our silence would permit other demons to take our ghost's place. It was a silence that could have been deadly to our faith, our home, and our family.

An out-of-state subscriber stopped by one day to renew her subscription. As she chatted with us we learned she knew how to read palms. Soon every member of the staff had had his or her palm read, clinging to Martha's every word as she traced our head and heart lines, laughing when she noted the possibility of an affair or future fame or great wealth. It was fun, and several of us, myself included, bought books to pursue the study on our own. Mine were placed in a growing spiritualist library that had begun quite accidentally at a public auction when I had to buy several cartons of books to get the Civil War volumes I wanted. The spiritualist books, bleak and somber looking, had a certain "to heck with organized religion" feel to them that spoke to me at that point in my life, and I gave over a whole shelf in the den to them. Friends and, eventually, the daughter of our departed ghost, spent nerve-prickling late hours discussing their contents—life after death, talks with the dead, psychic happenings. I don't think any of us actually read the books, but we drew from their presence for our conversations.

And when Georgette, who sometimes helped with the mailing, produced her Ouija board, I enjoyed helping her ask questions. She was an Aries, I a Libra, opposites on the zodiac. The chemistry worked well. We asked Ouija for election predictions before the returns came in, and by morning we knew it had been more accurate than the networks' early forecasts. Buoyed by our success, we spent many late night hours with it, asking it to predict our own futures and those of friends who eagerly crowded around to watch the planchette swirl across the board under our fingers. But we soon tired of the silly questions. By then we already knew I would write a book within two years and that Georgette's life would change within six months. We were ready for more. We again turned to Ouija, because, after all, hadn't it been right about the elections? Hadn't it told us that Polly and Willy were having marital problems even before we saw Polly coming out of the tavern with her lover? Even before news of Willy's indescretions rocked the community? The "mystifying oracle" was a pretty smart little board, we decided, and we turned to it more often.

Then one day Georgette asked it to identify the person to whom we were talking, the one really guiding the planchette. I was unaware anyone was supposed to be in charge; I simply thought that plastic board knew the answers, and I stared in amazement as the planchette spelled out the name of her dead brother and spewed forth answers that seemed to satisfy her. The replies quieted any nagging suspicion I had that the people operating the board really supplied the answers, however indirectly. Georgette was new in the community, and I knew nothing of her family. There was no way the board could have received any vibrations from me, and if it received them only from her, it succeeded in transmitting a very strong message.

Then one day came an exceptionally strong message. In response to a question about her brother, the planchette first balked, then rapidly spelled out, "Go to hell."

We gasped and stared at the planchette. It refused to move. "A bad spirit took over," she said, and we attempted to dismiss the frightening incident from our minds. Later, in the security of my own den, we repeated our attempts. This time Georgette was able to communicate with her brother and was pleased with the answers she received. Since ours was the house in which our ghost had once lived, I asked to speak to him, and, after some waiting, the planchette noted he was in control. The "ghost" said he'd left our house because we had laughed, that he'd really meant us no harm but had merely wanted to get our attention.

Later, we received a longer message from him: "Look for the nun with the jug." This took many questions to clarify, but we finally learned the nun was a hollow figurine, containing Spanish coins. We were told that the figurine was in our cistern, a no longer used, jug-shaped, cement-covered excavation at the back of the house not three feet from the door through which the footsteps stomped the night the "ghost" fled our house.

"What else is there?" we asked, and he replied, "Mice, water, and bugs."

We persisted. "What else?"

"Me," came the cryptic reply.

We didn't find a body or a nun in the cistern, but one of the spiritualist books yielded the information that ghosts frequently reside in abandoned wells near old houses. Neither Georgette nor I knew this, but Ouija did. The board had convinced us of its accuracy. We had found something new and interesting, and we pursued it with vigor.

New lines of questions led us to "talk" to Frederick the Great of Prussia who told us a great deal about Catherine the Great of Russia, describing her lovers and the deaths of her husband and son. We were astounded, because until then, neither of us had read about Catherine. We had to read several books before we learned as much as Ouija told us about her, except for one thing: I was, Ouija insisted, her reincarnation.

I was no longer worried about my severed church relations. I stayed up nights studying biographies of Catherine, liking little of what I read. I didn't want to be her reincarnation, but the thought was more fascinating than selling advertising and describing Sunday dinners, and I read on, taking a lot of teasing from my family about "my past."

My present, however, was filled with long hours in both offices and weekly after-hour sessions with Georgette and Ouija. Since the vibrations were stronger at our house than anywhere else, she often left the board there, and sometimes Doug and I experimented with it. He, too, is an Aries. But it was not the same. Doug was not amused by the board and its predictions. Whenever he tried to use it, the planchette spelled out unreadable messages until it finally gave us one that startled us both: "I hate you."

"I hate you, too!" he cried.

That incident should have served as adequate warning about the board that didn't always give nice messages, but it went unheeded. I decided Doug was just nervous because of his new medication and made certain he wasn't around when Georgette and I conducted our "discussions." No sense upsetting him.

But we did. When he was six and the Ouija board operated by his own mother was telling him it hated him, Doug could only react in fear and tears. As a loving mother determined to bring order into her son's life, I was certainly confusing him by my continued use of the plastic sorcerer. The ghost that so long had frightened him had been replaced by pills and something equally disturbing. How God must have wept at a parent who insisted on pursuing what the Bible clearly states is evil in the sight of the Lord, praying all the while, "Please, God, don't let us go too far."

But we did go too far. We liked talking to Frederick the Great, a man we now called Fred. We enjoyed hearing how many reincarnations we each had had. Still, I often felt the seances got into areas in which we had no business, areas that left me feeling dirty and intruding. I can't describe the feeling. It was one of disgust, one that truly asked, "What am I doing here?" Perhaps it was one asked by God as another warning as I continued to follow the urgings of the fascinating sorcerer.

Since Georgette and I were novices, we were delighted to find a friend far more adept with Ouija than we. It was Marty. Years earlier, she and Russ had established "guides" who conducted them through various planes of existence, even venturing past death and talking to spirits on "the other side." This wasn't done in the light-hearted manner we'd enjoyed while talking to our ghost or to Fred, and I watched with bonechilling horror as Ouija took Marty and Russ back to ancient Egypt and their lives there.

A Bible lay on the table around which we were seated. Its presence seemed inconsequential. "How does this relate?" I asked.

"Notice how religious Ouija is," Marty said. And she appeared to be right. Outside of telling Doug it hated him and telling Georgette and me to go to hell, it had said little that could be construed as off-color or morally suggestive. It frequently expressed absolute displeasure with smoking or drinking, spelling out admonitions to those who had those habits.

There were five of us at the seance, and my turn to get a guide never came. I wanted to get out into fresh air and sunshine although Marty's house was spotless.

"That's not for me," I told Loren later.

He laughed and replied, "You're hooked."

He was wrong, thank God.

But, in spite of my revulsion, I take no credit for stopping the seances. That must go to Nancy, who was not present because she did not believe in such things. She was our "religious" friend, the one for whom we said grace when she came to supper. She gave a book to the five of us involved in the seances that described the horrors of Ouija boards. The others read the book and made their decisions; as for me, I don't remember the name of it. I read a part of my copy before relegating it to the coffee table. Instead of finishing it, I read *The Exorcist* and found great similarity between the events that launched the little girl into a living hell and what the five of us had been doing in the comfort of one person's living room. And I reread 1 John 4:1-3: "Beloved, do not believe every spirit, but test the spirits to see whether they are of God; for many false prophets have gone out into the world. By this you know the Spirit of God: every spirit which confesses that Jesus Christ has come in the flesh is of God, and every spirit which does not confess Jesus is not of God. This is the spirit of antichrist, of which you heard that it was coming, and now it is in the world already."

The message was loud and clear: What we had been doing was sin, an abominable trespass against the God in whom we believed with all our hearts and souls. In seeking an entertaining escape from a heavy and grueling schedule, we had inadvertently turned to the father of lies. We prayed God would forgive us as we brought the seances to a screeching halt.

We also prayed that this time we would be on guard against letting another demon take the place of the one we were casting out. In Luke, Jesus tells a parable about a man from whom an evil spirit had been cast. The spirit later returned to the man, and finding the man's life empty, invited other evil spirits to join him in filling the void. We had inadvertently cast the ghost out of our lives but had not filled the void. Instead of allowing Christ to fill our hearts, we had, in effect, hung out a "Space Available" sign that permitted a far more destructive demon to enter. And regardless of how they are touted, never believe for a moment that Ouija boards are harmless little games sold in toy departments. They are the work of the devil himself, containing misleading spirits who disrupt family and friends and who frighten a little boy already doing battle with a condition he cannot understand.

It is unthinkable that I should have subjected Doug to this.

There were no more seances, no more palm-reading sessions, no more horoscopes. The two Ouija boards were burned. "It was nothing but a bit of plastic," Marty said later. "I'd cherished that thing in moves all over the United States, had grown attached to it, depended on it. It went up in a puff of smoke and was gone."

During this time of seances, my office had become a meeting place for Christians of every denomination and every degree of faith, people not locked in spiritual closets, people who feared something alien had entered my life although no mention of the seances was ever made in either edition of the *News*. But they felt the presence of something evil and had come to help.

I know now this was the hand of God reaching out to me, but then I was merely disturbed by their overtures and frightened by a new horror: While we had become so involved in the occult, Nancy, the friend we had forsaken because we knew her faith would not permit her to attend our seances, had been stricken with cancer.

I'll never forget the expression on her face the day she came into my office, slumped into the visitor's chair and said, "The doctor just found a mass."

"A mass of what?" I asked stupidly as I looked up from my proofreading.

"We won't know until after the surgery," she said, her face pale and drawn.

"Is there anything we can do to help?"

"Pray," she whispered.

The five of us who had once participated in seances visited Nancy as often as we could, unable to speak of the verdict the doctor pronounced after surgery, unable to bear the thought of what would be. Ruby joined the church. "Nancy's faith has moved me to it," she announced, and we rejoiced with her even as we watched cancer consume Nancy's tiny body and saw the radiation treatments consume her hair and eyebrows.

Long unaccustomed to praying *for* things since my answered

prayers had too often been filled with tears, I turned to God for strength and comfort both for Nancy and myself. I could not understand why He needed her, but He obviously did because, despite a gigantic circle of prayer chains upholding her with their love, concern, and prayers, she died with a smile after months of pain and suffering.

"God moves in strange and wondrous ways," we were told at the funeral where Hattie and I clung together and wept at our loss. I could not understand why God had taken Nancy when her husband and daughters so desperately needed her, but for the first time in my life, I did not retreat from a threat to my faith. "There is a reason for everything," the minister said.

I remembered a woman who had survived the tornadoes that ripped our area saying, "God does strange things to bring us together. The good of the tornado is that at least one woman now attends church who never did before. She came to help prepare food for the workers and has been with us ever since."

I rejected that theory, but I watched in wonder as one after another of my friends turned to Christ. The Ouija board owners have become extremely active church workers. In pre-seance days they were irregular in attendance and seldom took part. Now they are Bible students and teachers whose abilities are being recognized outside their own churches. All except Ruby. She's dropped out of church. "God let me down," she says. "He took Nancy in spite of my prayers, in spite of the prayers of everyone who knew her. A just God would not do that."

Poor Ruby, I thought, using God as a talisman, a good luck charm, but I shuddered to realize how often I did the same thing, and I shared her disappointment even as I kept saying, "There has to be a reason."

I still cannot accept the idea that God took Nancy because He wanted us to rejoin a church, but I rejoice and give thanks for her courage to speak against what we were doing. In her own quiet way, Nancy helped us end a practice that would have eventually destroyed the order we were attempting to bring into Doug's life and even our relationship with God. How grateful we are for having had a friend concerned enough to become involved.

My own renunciation of things occult was slower than that of the Ouija board owners. It was done with a great deal of help from the people who continued to call and to a sudden urge to write a series of articles about various Bible study groups in our area. That these people and that so-called "urge" were also gifts of God did not occur to me until much later. All I knew then was that I wanted to learn more about other faiths, denominations other than my own which does not believe in demon spirits. Many of the people I interviewed believe demons can move into houses, that, because of my association with the occult, one had moved into our house in the form of a ghost even though his arrival preceded the Ouija board by several years. "Either you or someone who lived there before permitted a demon to invade your house," a librarian told me. "Burn those spiritualist books," a beautician said as she gave me a tract telling me how to rid my life of the demon that lurked not only between the books' covers but in my home, that cherished haven of tranquility to which we fled from our busy schedules.

"But I love books," I protested. "I don't believe in book burnings. The idea is repugnant."

"Burn them," she insisted, using as her biblical basis Acts 19:19: "And a number of those who practice magic arts brought forth their books together and burned them in the sight of all; and they counted the value of them and found it came to fifty thousand pieces of silver."

I looked at the books. They had cost less than fifteen or twenty dollars, not fifty thousand pieces of silver, but they had taken up too much space in my life. Resolutely, I scooped them off the shelf and into a box . . . but I could not burn them. I simply could not hold a match to the books that had influenced my life so much, even though the influence was not a positive one. Instead, I had Todd take them to school to give one of his teachers who in turn would give them to an area seminary.

"Maybe they can study the bad with the good," I told the teacher later.

"Those books," he said. "The devil must have been very pleased with them."

The books had been mine and they had influenced my life. Now they were gone, but were there any demons left lurking?

I took out the tract the beautician had given me and read the injunction for the devil to get out of my life once and for all. I read it three times. And I meant every word of it. This was not an exorcism but a simple act of faith. I wanted God in my life, not the devil or anything that even resembled his work.

And with that act of faith, I knew without question we were at a turning point. Bob, my aborted return to college, our realization that we couldn't print four papers, Doug's affliction, the occult—unpleasant topics we had shied from in print, that could have helped others had we the courage to share—had all come to a point from which there could be no turning. We were no longer the same Loren and Ann we had been the day the presses didn't stop, the day my answered prayer had become reality. We were so changed that there was little resemblance to those timid souls who had marched into a print shop unprepared and undertaken roles about which we had no understanding. Our faith in God had been strong that fateful day, but we had weakened it by securely locking it in closets of our own making. We had become closet Christians, separating ourselves from God's church, His people. We had become fearful, thinking that if we made any overtures that appeared "religious" people would brand us hypocrites. Yet God had sustained us every step, every Thursday of the way. He held us up and strengthened us when our own feeble reserves failed.

Doug was well on his way to living a normal life, two of my former Ouija mates had turned to their churches with new fervor, the others were turning to new vocations. I was the person whose wildest dreams had become a reality, the one whose prayers had been answered with the ownership of not one paper but two.

Now was the time to change my outlook and possibly the papers themselves.

Never very good at expressing my deepest feelings without tears, I groped for a way to tell Loren that I wanted us to change directions with the papers. The words wouldn't come, but the tears did, and as I blotted them away, I blurted out a direct quote from one of the squibs tacked to my bulletin board. "If life hands you a lemon, make lemonade."

"I'd rather make it a job shop," he said. The role of publisher had been a disappointment for him, but he had discovered a new love in the smell and feel of the printer's ink that saturated his clothes and covered his knuckles.

"So you print, I'll run the papers," I said grandly.

"Someone has to print them and someone has to sell half the advertising," he reminded.

"True," I conceded, "but let's see if we can't work out something."

It was a statement that sounded promising even as I knew there was little immediate chance of its being fulfilled. I still had a lot to learn about answered prayer.

11

Paste-Up Is Easy

"**T**om just quit," Loren said as he arrived early for our Monday lunch date, the only shared time we spent away from home or shop.

His words had a chilling effect. Tom had been the backbone of both the newspaper and the job departments. Without a Linotype operator, we would be in a very vulnerable position.

"You told me it's time to change the direction of the papers, so maybe this is a sign to do it," Loren said. "Something will work out. God's been with us every step of the way so far—at least every step we've let Him—and He'll find us an operator if He wants us to have one."

"That's right," I said, silently giving thanks for Loren's calm attitude, and praying he was right.

And, as He had done in the past, God provided another operator: Doreen, mother of seven and a country-trained worker who had once owned her own weekly.

Much as we liked Doreen, we knew instinctively she would not be with us long; soon she and her clan would move on. Before she left, however, we wanted to compile a long list of possible applicants for her job.

The result of our inquiries was frightening. There were no more applicants. Offset reproduction had made great inroads into former letterpress shops and its effect was being felt in the training schools. "Sorry, we have no graduates to recommend," they replied, and one added a poignant note, "If you hear of anyone who wants to attend our school, please send us his name."

The change we sought for our papers coincided with Tom's resignation and Doreen's coming coincided with the change we sought. She gave her notice eight weeks after she arrived, and we knew there would be no replacement. We had a choice—sink without an operator or swim with an entirely new system. There was no alternative but to seek the latter.

Offset had to be the answer. Greatly refined since we purchased the *News,* offset represented a cold type system of setting type, one that could be done, if necessary, on a typewriter. Where we had relied on heavy mats that Loren used as forms in casting ad layouts, offset required only scissors and a paste pot. Offset relied on photography and demanded the use of a darkroom and presses that made our tired press look like a fugitive from the dark ages. Offset was neat and clean as opposed to the inky, greasy system we had used for years. And offset scared us.

Loren carried the electric typewriters into the office and called a staff conference, which included the two of us and an office girl named Sarah. "Type the copy twenty-three spaces wide," he said, "and leave slash marks at the end of the line if you need to fill in space and "½" marks if you have to squeeze."

"This is where we started back in high school," I sighed.

"Oh, but the rest of it will be different," he said. "I've contracted for a weekly in the next county to print our paper. All we have to do is take them the paste-up and they'll do the rest. And the press they have is something else."

He was so enthusiastic that I sat down and typed twenty-three-space lines from the Twenty-third Psalm: "The Lord is my shepherd, I shall not want; he makes me lie down in green pastures. He leads me beside still waters; he restores my soul. He leads me in paths of righteousness for his name's sake." Properly expanded and justified in column form, the message was comforting, and our green pastures looked more enticing when I decided the type, while not as impressive as that used by the daily papers, wasn't all that bad.

The switch to offset, while relieving us of the need for a Linotype operator, would mean putting out to pasture both the ancient press and the Linotype. The switch would plunge us right back to the first year of another three-year program. And it meant doing something even more frightening, something we'd talked of but stalled doing for years: the two papers had to become one, because there was no way we could justify two seventy-mile round trips to the printer each week. Our own one-two vote had been decided by absolute necessity.

We feared what would happen when the merged *News* hit the stands. In the meantime, however, we had to re-learn page make-up done without make-ups, turtles, quoins, or chases.

Our hard-learned knowledge consisted of nothing. Indeed it seemed to have walked out the door with Doreen. We found ourselves armed with hot wax, students of an art called paste-up.

"Paste-up is easy," a printer told us, and I had to agree it was cleaner than letterpress had been. Where I formerly had worn old clothes swathed in heavy shop aprons on press day, I could now report for work in white pants and pastel sweaters and go home clean. The seventy-five pound forms were replaced by make-up sheets ruled in pale blue. The copy fitted neatly into the columns, held firmly in place by the hot wax. It was going to be a great system, I told myself, trying to remember all the advice I had read about looking back as I surveyed expensive equipment rendered obsolete. I prayed I wouldn't cry as I pieced together a brand new paper that bore the proud new flag we'd had designed especially for the *new News,* a merger of two newspapers totaling more than a century of existence and representing two towns still years from agreement on a school system. My hands shook so hard I could scarcely control them, but I thanked God for the new start and prayed for guidance and wisdom to deal calmly with any rough situations that might arise.

It was a time of change, a time of rejoicing, a time of nervousness, and a time of sorrow. The first obituary under the new banner was Sophie Palmer's. Our staunch friend and ally had been felled by a bad heart she had seldom mentioned as she tried "to run ahead of the pack." No one found a bottle of whiskey in her house, much to Hattie's joy, so no one ever knew if she really had a teaspoon full every night or if that was another of her interesting tales. The change we sought for our paper coincided with many changes in our lives. Our personal existence had undergone many upheavals in the past few years, none more severe than the unexpected death of Loren's father as we rushed to put out a special Christmas edition. Called from the press by his father's co-workers, Loren helped volunteers lift his only parent—cancer had claimed his mother years before—to the waiting hearse, then returned to print the paper all night and during all the minutes between calling hours and the funeral itself. Always on Thursday took on new meaning as we choked back tears and worked out our sorrow. Now we did the same for Sophie.

It was also a time for surprise. Four pages of type had weighed three hundred pounds. Now I could put the paste-up for a sixteen-page paper in a box, and the whole package weighed only a few ounces. And even I, the person to whom mechanics mean nothing, was impressed with the operation of the press when I made my first trip to the printer. In less than two hours, page negatives were shot, metal plates burned, and the paper printed. Even more miraculous was the fact that the paper came off, not four pages at a time, but twelve or sixteen or even thirty-two or forty-eight at a time, all assembled, folded, and ready for mailing. The back-breaking work of folding, sorting, and collating was gone forever. It was a miracle beyond my wildest comprehension, and on that fateful Thursday I needed all the miracles God had to offer because I was scared to death, nearly frozen with fear at what community reaction might be when the new publication reached the stands.

The warts of one town previously reported predominantly to its own readers were now there for the other town's readers to see. And they, in turn, knew their problems would be read by "those people at the other end." A petition to fire the marshal in one town was read avidly by readers in the other, while one town was delighted that the other was so embroiled in a discussion over sewer plans that one of the leading citizens purchased a two-page advertisement in which he said he personally would carry buckets of any "slop" that backed into his basement to the front doors of every town board member. And the school situation, uppermost in most people's minds, could be discussed in letters to the editor that would prove threatening to both towns. We prayed that no one would panic.

"I don't want to know what those people are doing," Norman P. Sandler said, and he started another free publication to promote "his" town. It lasted six weeks, but in the meantime readers protested that the *News* contained nothing of interest to "their" town, although we had deleted nothing from either paper. It was all there—the columns of news gleaned from past issues, *Odds and Ends,* the community news, births, deaths, weddings, the who-ate-what-and-with-whom items. Nothing was missing, but in adding another set of names we had created something threatening, a loss of identity.

"It's obvious you favor one school since you found it more economical to publish a single paper," Marty Singleton wrote, although she refused to let us print her letter when we reminded her we never withheld names from letters to the editor.

"We've been friends for such a long time. Couldn't you make an exception for me?"

"Sorry," we said, not wanting to say no but wanting even less to set a precedent.

"But printing it with my name would be dangerous to a person in my position," she persisted. "What about my church and civic ties? People might be offended."

"If we print an editorial, everyone knows how we feel," we

replied. "Some are offended. It's a risk you have to take when you have a personal opinion."

"No thanks," Marty snapped. "Some friends you turned out to be." Another friendship wavered.

Ruby Pearl had what she considered to be a better idea. "What you really should do," she said, "is write an editorial about the school board member from the other end of the district. He doesn't think as Jim and I do."

"He just got on the board. Give him a chance," Loren said. It was a mild statement for the man who long ago had grown impatient with readers who demanded front page treatment for their news or who wanted to dictate their views through the editorial column. "Why don't you write an editorial?" came to engender the same reaction a plunger cast into a keg of dynamite brings, an explosion.

"Have you talked with him personally? He seems like a fair man," Loren said, but Ruby stomped off in a huff. No one needed to tell us what she and Jim would say the next time we called for advertising.

"This paper is the only common meeting ground the residents of this school corporation have," I told Loren. "There must be something we can do to help soothe the troubled waters."

"Once there were five high schools," he reminded me. "Now there are two. Both towns feel threatened. Combining the papers looks like consolidation, a loss of either town's individuality."

"There have been a lot of changes," I agreed, remembering the night fire poured from one of the former high schools reduced by consolidation to a junior high, the changes in the business communities in both towns and in those settlements also affected by consolidation. "There must be something we can do," I added.

"The paper is your baby," he said. "You do what you want to."

Loren's blunt statement coincided neatly with a meeting I had attended where I was alternately fascinated and repulsed by two women speakers, the first "libbers" I had met. The truth was, I already felt very liberated—free at last from the dirty, heavy job of making up pages "the old way" and from the pressures of two deadlines.

My response to the speakers was negative. I didn't like them, nor did I like their message. It was not an opinion shared by all, and the women's editor of a large daily found my thinking too provincial. "Go back home and find out what your women are doing besides midwifing sows and sewing," she snapped.

"Plenty," I said in a whisper, because, in truth, I knew little of what the people in our area were actually doing. I knew who was eating dinner with whom, but I'd been so busy with the nuts and bolts of the operation, so involved with turtles, quoins, and newsprint, I'd had little time to really know anyone outside the circle of friends cast asunder by a Ouija board. Other than my column, I had done little creative writing, certainly not the kind I longed for when we purchased the *News*. The camel caravan had almost been forgotten, the sophisticated reporter replaced by an innocent who despaired at our failure with Bob and who was openly shocked when Polly and Willy began separate affairs.

I decided the women's editor was right: I was too provincial, too protected. And I intended to remedy that situation with a series of articles about the people of our area.

12

Crafters, Spinners, and Doers

Could it be that this conversion to a new system and my desire to know more about our area's people were more of God's "coincidences?" It certainly appeared so, and I whispered thanks again as I experimented by moving parts of the paper around until I had opened a large news hole in the center of the paper. It would be perfect for a centerfold, not the kind that drew voyeurs and deviates, but one that reported on the good that people were doing. These centerfolds would be populated by the men and women who lived in our area and whose lives crossed ours. It was not a large beat, nor could it be considered a small one. The two towns our paper served each had a population of about one thousand, while the school corporation that encompassed both towns drew from three other townships. In all, our main concentration of readers lived in a 199-square-mile area, one hundred square miles smaller than New York City but with a population of slightly more than ten thousand. I didn't know how long it would take a camel caravan to cross the length and breadth of the district, but I knew from experience I could cover many miles in a few minutes with my bright red car, a purchase made the same week as the new camera that beckoned me into an unknown field of reporting.

It took all the courage I had to call my first subject and say, "You have an interesting hobby. How about letting me write an article about it?"

But when she said, "Yes," I was launched into a world of crafters, spinners, and doers that gave lie to my image of them as artsy-craftsy folk bent on making dolls from filter pads and given to sewing buttons on dust cloths arranged to look like little suits. It is a world from which I have yet to tire, a world filled with dedicated crafts people who know life is a bit less tedious if a little of each day or each week is spent creatively. It is a world from which there is satisfaction to be gained from creating miniature settings, dried flower arrangements, sculpting, carving, or painting porcelain dolls. The work may be more trying than his or her normal occupation, but it is something so far removed from what he does for a living, so totally different, so demanding, yet so rewarding that it is too important to be overlooked. It is the best therapy in the world, better by far than all the nerve tonics combined. Coupled with prayer and a strong faith in God, hobbies offer a balm for life's complexities, an escape from a world given over to computers.

No one was more surprised at my plans than Polly, who still dropped by to chat once in a while. I disapproved of her affair but remained silent. However, she sensed my internal frown and delighted in needling me about my limited outlook, our rural community. "It's so small, there's nothing to do or see," she said, waving her arm contemptuously at the downtown area.

"Except you and your boss sitting in the front window of the bar and then driving home by way of a motel," I wanted to say, but, instead, I smiled and defended ours as the ideal area in which to rear a family, in which to live and work. And I meant it. The rewards of weekly journalism were interesting; there were stimulating people in both towns.

"What do you expect to find?" Polly demanded. "What do you think you'll unearth if you storm the area with camera and notebook in hand that you haven't found sitting in your office or wallowing around in the ink and grime of the backshop?"

"I'm not sure," I said. "I'll just have to see what turns up."

"You going to have both men and women?" she demanded.

"Certainly. We want interesting people who are creative and imaginative. We don't care what color their skin is or if they're male or female, Protestant, Catholic, or Jew."

"That's dangerous," she said. "We live right in the buckle of the Bible Belt, right where it gets tight. Someone will get you for saying things like that."

She was right. We were not without prejudice, but I was too stubborn to admit it.

"What do you expect to find?" she repeated.

"Who knows?" I said. "Maybe a Bible Belt reaction to the woman's movement. Maybe not. I'm not sure at all. I just want to learn what people are doing besides eating Sunday dinner with each other and dying."

"For one thing, they sometimes rape each other, and child abuse isn't unheard of. A friend of my neighbor girl had an abortion last week. You might report that."

"If you've done one abortion, you've done them all," I said, quoting an editor I'd heard at a meeting. "This is going to be different."

"Well, it should be interesting," she conceded as she added one final barb, "but don't be disappointed with what the women are doing. Most of them are either at the drugstore having coffee or home watching soap operas."

Contrary to Polly's prediction, few of the women I encountered were having coffee at the drugstore or watching television. Some didn't own sets, and if they had one, they seldom watched. They were too busy creating to have time to be bothered by anything so mundane as television.

As much to convince myself as Polly, I conducted interviews early in the morning, late at night, and more often than not sandwiched between editing and paste-up responsibilities. The result was a kaleidoscope as multi-colored as a housewife's vibrant quilts and as many-faceted as the gems the rural mail carrier polished in his lapidary.

"I know a girl who had an abortion last year who's dying of cancer of the cervix," Polly said after an article about a woman who makes dolls appeared in the *News*. "Why don't you do something about botched up abortions?"

"People are tired of reading that kind of stuff. That's the realm of papers with staffs large enough to back investigative reporting."

"It's news."

"A weekly's role is to concentrate on local events—to give space for what might even be called 'the unimportant,' " I said.

"The girl graduated here last year."

"You report one abortion, you've done them all," I requoted.

"But this isn't all of them. It involves a girl everyone knows."

"That's another good reason not to do it. Nothing can be accomplished by causing her or her family any more heartache than they've already suffered."

"Not even if you prevent another girl from going through the same thing?"

It was a good question, and I faltered. "It would still hurt the girl," I said. "Even if we protected her anonymity, she could be hurt."

"I say you're giving your readers a one-sided view of life," Polly persisted.

Hattie Hooper, however, agreed with me. "I think the center-folds are fine just the way they are. I'm sick of reading about abortions. I don't believe in them. Give me good news any time."

"Both of you are seeing life through rose-colored glasses," Polly said.

"Maybe so, but I'm tired of reading about abortions, rape, murder, liquor . . ." Hattie said, ticking off her dislikes on her fingers. "I like to know there are still good people in the world, people who make rag dolls to keep alive family traditions, people who use their God-given talents to their fullest." Hattie, who mothered her three granddaughters as she once had Nancy and who protected her son-in-law even as he turned more and more to the bottle, still had not renewed her subscription. It was interesting to know she continued to read the *News,* that she found something to her liking.

The rewards of this type of writing were many. A good reporter never accepts gifts from anyone, especially the subject of an interview, but that's a motto hard to keep when the gifts are given by friends. All of us enjoyed the flowers, goat milk, bags of carrots, plaques, candy, honey, and countless other little gifts that were tucked into my camera bag.

Perhaps the best reward of all, however, was seeing the pleasure that came to each interviewee as he or she was given the centerfold for the week. It gave new meaning to Proverbs 3:27: "Do not withhold good from those to whom it is due, when it is in your power to do it." I was the editor, the decisions were mine, and I delighted in sharing readers' lives with each other, even as in doing so, I came to understand better the reason Cora and Vera and so many others liked the little personal items, the Mr.-and-Mrs.-Lyle-Mason-were-Sunday-dinner-guests-of-Mr.-and-Mrs.-Clifton-Jones type stories. My attempts to squelch these were actually withholding the good of seeing their name in print for those readers.

"I didn't know we had so many talented people in our area," Norman P. Sandler said. It was a compliment that included both towns, not just one, and I felt my efforts amply repaid even as I knew I had grown with each interview. At heart an introvert, I had to force myself to call the people and meet with them. It was not the same as doing rewrites, dashing off an *Odds and Ends* column or preparing summaries of school board meetings. Light years from camel-back journalism, it was also far removed from what I had been doing. This was actually going forth and meeting our readers one on one. It was the most challenging and most rewarding writing I ever did.

I had also joined a state women's press group at the urging of a friend who thought I would benefit from an exchange of ideas with fellow journalists. I found the meetings stimulating and provocative. It was at one of them that I became so angry at a pair of women's libbers and the ensuing exchange of ideas with a woman's editor that I launched my own Bible Belt crusade to learn what was going on besides school consolidation. When the club's annual writing contest was announced, I decided to live dangerously by submitting columns, centerfolds, page layouts, editorials, everything in which I had a hand, which, in reality, was all the paper except the classified page—the pride of Loren's life outside of the job department. Months later, Florence, a good friend from a daily newspaper, and I drove to Indianapolis for the awards luncheon.

It was a delightful day, despite the rain and drizzle, and when the awards were announced I was ecstatic—five first place citations!

Amid congratulations and best wishes from journalists from all over the state, we waved goodbye and prepared to drive home. That's when I learned I had left the car's lights on. The battery was dead. Ten minutes and $4.50 later, we were on our way, contemplating how we would celebrate with our families.

I didn't have to look far to find mine. All three were in the kitchen, dribs of ham salad and pieces of potato chips indicating they had not starved while I was gone. They had received a list of winners and already were beaming when I entered. Amid congratulations were hugs and kisses. It was a wonderful moment, too precious to be broken by mention of the battery, but I've never been noted for my timing.

"For that much money they should have thrown in the jumper cable," Loren said. "And that reminds me, you goofed in this week's paper when you said 'a man' noticed Lyle Mason's barn fire. You should have been more specific and said it was George Wilson. And what happened to the news of the Chamber of Commerce basketball game?"

Todd was the most excited. "Wow! I can hardly wait to tell the kids. Gary has been bragging about his prize-winning cow. I have a prize-winning mother!"

"I'll make a pizza to celebrate," I said.

"I have an appointment," Loren said.

"I'll fix popcorn for the boys and me," I said, but my words were cut short by a telephone call from their uncle wanting to know if they'd like to accompany his family to a movie. Their whoops indicated a movie was far more exciting than popcorn with mother.

"Tell them to bring Ronnie down here. I'll take care of him while they're gone," I said. After all, someone should be there for my celebration, and my six-month-old nephew would fill the bill nicely.

Ronnie watched in fascination as I sorted the week's laundry—prize winner or not, we needed clean clothes—but after a time the novelty wore off and his bottle didn't suit and he was dry. Worst of all, I seemed to have lost my ability to soothe a crying baby. Finally, in desperation, I showed him my gold-edged prize certificates. He took a long, hard look at them, emitted two giant burps and snuggled against my shoulder, sound asleep.

Sitting in the quiet house, listening to the tick of the clocks, the hum of the washer and dryer, and the quiet breathing of the sleeping baby, his downy head still pushed against my cheek, I pondered my day of fame and limelight and knew that no matter what else ever happened to me, I was not a complete failure—I was as good as a prize cow, and my writing certificates were the best thing for gas since the discovery of baking soda.

13

Parts Missing

For more than 300 Tuesdays, a maroon and white car stopped in front of the *News* office, its horn honking, its engine revving with impatience. "Joy's here!" someone would shout, and one or more of us would run to greet her. With a quick smile, an infectious giggle, and her bright blue eyes snapping with humor, she would say, "Get in quick. It's too hot to stand out there." Or, "Get in before you freeze to death." The weather outside her car was never right; she longed for the companionship of friends, inside, with her.

"I've got a lot to tell you," she would say as we watched her carefully remove straight pins from pages of news that smelled faintly of bayberry.

It was only at first that we really noticed she had no legs. After that, the horn merely announced the arrival of a community correspondent. Certainly it did not indicate the presence of a handicapped person, because Joy refused to admit she had a problem. She drove her own car by using special hand controls and was able to get in and out of it by herself. Once, while Loren was still recuperating from surgery and I was working late in the shop, I heard a swish behind me and turned to find her wheeling around the Linotype.

"Why didn't you honk?" I asked.

"You're busier than I am. Besides, I wanted to see what the place looks like. She investigated every corner of the building and, refusing my offers of assistance, departed as rapidly as she had come.

Visiting her home, which she maintained herself "because I don't want anyone to have to do anything for me," I marveled at her abilities, her mobility. "I can do anything except hang draperies," she said, but the lack caused her no end of dismay.

"It's nothing," she said when I complimented her. "Anyone could do it."

"You're wrong. I'm not sure I could adjust to life without legs."

"Not now, maybe," she said. "You have a husband and children and a job. People need you. No one needed me when my legs were amputated, and it was easier to adjust. The thing to remember is, when life knocks you down, pick yourself up and fight back."

I often pleaded with her to let me write a feature about her. "You're an inspiration to everyone who knows you. Let's share it with others."

But she would only laugh. "No one wants to read about a funny person like me. I've only done what anyone else would do—I've learned to live with my problems."

She remembered us with gifts, often of her own making. "Thought you might enjoy this," she would say. "Everyone needs something to pick them up once in a while."

Everyone needs something, someone. If the life knocks you down, pick yourself up. These were her messages. When we felt down in the dumps, we thought of Joy and counted our blessings. If our legs hurt, we remembered she had none but that her indomitable spirit more than made up for the loss of limbs. We counted our own good legs and our friendship with her among our treasured assets.

The call came on Sunday that the horn would not sound on Tuesday. Death had done what no mere amputations could ever do: our silver-haired friend was gone, felled by a heart attack during my traditional Sunday afternoon nap. The house was a shambles, and my disposition was on a par with a hungry mountain lion. The boys had fought and now Doug was outdoors and Todd was upstairs dreaming of a ten-speed bicycle. Loren had returned to the shop in an attempt to catch up on some of his printing. When the telephone rang, I snarled to myself, "As soon as I'm done talking, I'm going back to sleep." Instead, shocked, I found myself cleaning the house, folding clothes, and thinking of Joy. If life knocks you down, pick yourself up and fight back, she had said.

I told Todd that Joy was gone. His face paled and he blinked, but then, as if remembering her message, he left the catalogs behind and fixed his old bicycle and startled me even further by volunteering to accompany Doug on his first bicycle ride, a trip that brought the younger boy so much pleasure he pleaded for a second. "No," Todd said gently but firmly. "It's time to do chores." But when the calves were fed, he helped his little brother fly his new model airplane and then tuned in Doug's favorite television program. There was not a cross word between them, and I marveled at their accomplishments, only then discovering I had cleaned the house, folded the laundry and put it away, emptied the sweeper bag, and made a batch of popcorn.

"No one has yet printed a handbook to tell editors how to write obituaries of friends and relatives," I told readers in my column that week, "and until they do, all we can say is, 'Goodbye, Joy. We loved you.' "

"I didn't know her, but she must have been a wonderful person," readers wrote. "Makes you stop and count your blessings, doesn't it?" Hattie asked, and Polly, who could not stand Hattie, blinked back tears and agreed.

But the handicapped were also counting their blessings. From the determined third grader who played basketball with one leg held aloft by a strap from his waist to help correct a bone deficiency to the one-armed cheerleader to the one-armed aerobatic pilot and the farmer facing life with only half an arm, all were grateful to be alive and doing what they wanted to do. Joy went to her grave confident she had met life head-on by picking herself up and fighting back after life had knocked her down.

It was the same spirit I found when I interviewed anyone who was crippled. They were facing life as it was and, in the process, enjoying themselves with new-found hobbies.

"I hurry to get my work done so I can have time to play," a polio victim said as he showed Doug and me around his jeweler's shop and demonstrated his homemade toys built from scraps.

It was a statement I'd heard many hobbyists make, but in his instance it had certain overtones of Joy's philosophy.

It was a philosophy shared by Forrest Meredith. The father of seven sons, Meredith was a farmer used to working long, hard hours in the field. He was determined no accident would dampen his enthusiasm for living, that there is a reason for all things and that the hand of God was involved in his struggle to live a normal, productive life after a cornpicker accident cost him his right arm and two-thirds of the use of his left hand and arm.

"I knew while I was still in the picker that the hand of God was involved," he said. "That feeling and the excitement of wanting to know where it would lead helped strengthen me during the months in the hospital."

During his long convalescence in a Chicago research hospital, a therapist introduced him to leather working and later to ceramic tile crafts. "The ceramics were okay," he said in reminiscence, "but I really liked the leather. It took me four weeks to put together a belt made out of leather loops. It took me six days just to fold the first four loops."

By the time he returned to the farm, he had spent many hours in therapy, and leather working was still his favorite pastime. Now, three years later, he had converted a bedroom of the family home into a leather shop that boasted a heavy-duty sewing machine and other tools of his trade. Although he usually wore a prosthetic arm equipped with a hook, he had come to consider his real second hand an old-fashioned stitching horse that held his projects while he worked on them, and that allowed him to tighten the grip with foot pedals.

His farmer's eye for nature's beauty had helped him become even more of an artist as he continued to master his craft. When his wife admired a snakeskin he found, he made it into an attractive belt for her. A wallet for his son bore a picture of the boy's favorite tractor, and the son of a friend was given an attaché case bearing a full-color eagle on a blue ground.

"But I still get discouraged sometimes," he confessed. "I have to keep busy because the busier I am, the less frequent are the periods of depression."

And he had added new interests, including work at a local workshop for mentally and physically handicapped youngsters. A volunteer supervisor in the wood shop, he encouraged the boys' abilities as he helped them master the use of saws and woodworking equipment. "It's a challenge," he said, "but I like challenges." And as Art Swango had mastered flying, boating, and motorcycling with the use of one arm, so was Forrest Meredith regaining his ability to drive farm tractors and the family car. "I can master anything with power steering," he said, and he's still doing it.

Life knocked him down, but God helped Forrest Meredith pick himself up. "I had to," he said, "because I can still feel the hand of God guiding me every step of the way."

It was the same hand of God we felt in our weekly struggles with newsprint, ink, and type, but, unlike Forrest, we could not often speak of it. But we felt it and cherished it, drawing strength from it as we gave thanks to the God who had turned us outward into the world of people with parts missing who were meeting life so confidently and so full of love. They had much to give and they were doing so cheerfully and freely, no strings attached. They had laid their lives on God's altar and in doing so had become more nearly whole than we closet Christians who had two arms, two legs, and used them to carry our burdens instead of our joys.

14

Bible Belt Bushwhackers

The hand of God that supported Forrest Meredith in his struggle to be independent sustained Loren and me as we continued our personal search for meaning in a world punctuated with deadlines, printer's ink, and basketball teams waiting to have their pictures taken. Ours had become a world of advertising for which we had no stomach, basketball for which we have never experienced the thrill Hoosiers are supposed to feel, and school board stories that, while not as colorful as some of the book-burning ones of surrounding communities, were nevertheless stimulating because of the continued one-two school controversy.

Our once WASP farming communities had changed, and there would be no turning back. Appalachians who had come to the area seeking employment in the foundries, chicken dressing plants, and factories had become solid citizens who expressed fear as others joined their ranks, and as Mexicans with no visas and no work papers put still others out of work. Border patrol cars full of workers being returned home became common sights, although we are thousands of miles from the border.

Fear made it difficult for some people to open up about their favorite hobbies. "If anyone knew I had this, I'd never be able to sleep a wink," more than one subject said. "Someone would steal it for sure."

One of the most fascinating couples I ever interviewed, retirees with a penchant for history who recreated a Norman castle stone by stone, decided against my using the article, much as they enjoyed reading the advance copy. Years of labor had gone into creating their home, complete with towers, turrets, dungeons, and wine cellars, but they feared vandals could go from the armory entrance to the postern, creating instant havoc. Pictures of centuries-old doors and of a great room with a massive fireplace gather dust in my files because of a real terror, a terror ever as close as a car careening up the hill and shooting at the castle just because it was there. It was a fear that was real, that they had tasted as they watched snipers try to shoot out the few unbarricaded windows. "An attractive nuisance," their insurance agent called it, this towering edifice that was built as a tribute to centuries of architects and their skills. To the couple who built it, however, the castle served as a monument of their love for one another.

Law and order were still the objectives of both towns served by the *News.* Each town had to beef up its police force to handle the influx of drugs and larceny that moved in with returning servicemen, migrants, and the influx of city dwellers wishing to escape to communities where the pace was not as hectic. Many were surprised to find that street crime had preceded them, that drugs were used more frequently than in the areas from which they had fled. "You've got a lot bigger problem here than we ever had there," they said, but they stayed because crime still had not reached the near epidemic proportions it had there, and it was still safe to leave the doors unlocked—most of the time—and children and women were seldom molested on the streets.

The change the two towns feared would occur if the schools were consolidated occurred without consolidation. It was only a matter of time until two dozen of us watched black clouds roll away into a silvery, rain-streaked sunset as school board members wielded chrome-plated shovels and broke ground for a new high school to be built in neither town, but almost halfway between the two. Where corn once grew, steel girders were lifted into place as bulldozers rearranged topsoil and toppled an ancient set of buildings, a farmstead long a landmark. It was a time to be born and a time to die. A new era in education was dawning; the other would die except in the memories of those who would always remember how it had been when every town had its own high school, its own basketball team, and graduating classes that seldom numbered more than thirty.

The new school was well under construction when a tornado dealt a blow reminding us of the preacher's words in Ecclesiastes: "There is a time to plant, and a time to pluck up what is planted." The new school was untouched but the last remaining junior high was ripped apart and folded up like a used tissue. Additional classrooms were needed immediately, but one of the surviving schools had already been pushed past capacity after fire destroyed the other junior high. Children from three townships in kindergarten through grade twelve jammed into two buildings built to house children from one township. Portable classrooms scornfully referred to as sheep barns held the overflow. The other two schools were woefully inadequate to handle the influx of students from the tornado-ravaged building, and classes were conducted in a church basement, the fire station, and the pavilion at the Little League diamond.

No one, not even the most dedicated two-schooler, could deny that additional facilities were needed, and work on the new building intensified. The school superintendent presented me with a bright blue hard hat, and I roamed the construction site at will, taking pictures of the building some said would become nothing more than a sports complex while others envisioned it as a cathedral of learning that would send forth students better prepared than from any other school in the state.

In some respects, both prophecies have come true. While sports have often been stressed a bit more than we bookworms might like, the school has the highest average in the area of freshmen who later become graduating seniors. It has produced worthy citizens who are taking their places in the community or moving on to other areas, much as their parents and aunts and uncles did before them. The pessimists who thought their children would not have the opportunity to participate in sports and drama, have cheered lustily as not one basketball team but several, including girls, have taken to the floor, bringing home honors the previous schools failed to earn. The second year out, the football team, backed by a thousand screaming fans, many of whom had never seen the game played until it was introduced at the local "sports complex," romped its way to the state finals. And two years later, fans hugged each other in joy as the team won the state championship. Parents who did not know a handhold from a toehold have cheered for their sons' wrestling teams. Excellent dramatic productions have been presented on the stage that divides the commons from the lecture room. Swimmers make good use of the pool many described as a frill that could be done without, but that in reality has become the social connection between the two towns.

Virulent school board elections based on the one-two school question gave way to lackluster campaigns. The time for peace in the district had come.

We longed to think we had helped promote that peace, but we knew the credit was not ours. Nor did it belong to the people who took to the streets in protest and demonstration or to those who still could not find a good word to say about anyone in the other town. Much of the credit had to go to the students themselves. "Better is a poor and wise youth than an old and foolish king, who will no longer take advice," Ecclesiastes 4:13 tells us, and nowhere could there be found a better example of this than the last year the two schools existed. One of them did the impossible, its basketball team rising from a lackluster season to defeat the county seat's undefeated team for the sectional championship. Immediately, students from the second school, one whose team had done poorly all season, joined in celebration with their soon-to-be fellow classmates. A week of joint pep sessions and snake dances followed. Unfortunately, the team failed in the first game of the regional, but it did so in the presence of thousands of fans, many from the school up the road

that had also ceased to exist. Only a handful of the foolish be-
grudged either school's role. Basketball had won another round in
Hoosier politics.

"You'll either become drunkards or religious fanatics," Silas
Monroe had told us. Despite the stress placed on us by over-
crowded schedules, late night telephone calls, and demonstra-
tions, Old Demon Rum had not claimed us. Nor, unfortunately,
had religion. Still closet Christians, we were fearful of being
identified as believers by those who continued to pray for us,
people such as Hattie who openly admitted she thought we were
sinners for publishing police news and attending drug hearings.
If anyone mentioned religion to us we tended to recoil, to with-
draw within ourselves.

But there was a void in our lives, and we yearned to fill it, to
become God's movers and shakers, not disciples in hiding.
Perhaps that is why we continued seeking those who weren't
afraid to say, "I'm a Christian."

Certainly, the Bible Belt Bushwhackers were not hiding. They
were doing something and enjoying every minute of it. Some
were taking to the road as evangelists, others were less demon-
strative, but all had answered Jesus' call to discipleship. Once I
met them my life would never be the same again.

Many of these people, such as the ones who helped heal the
school corporation's wounds, were teenagers, and every Thursday
night anywhere from 30 to 110 of them crowded into the living
quarters of an abandoned backroad country store for Bible study.
Overflowing the donated couches and chairs, they spilled out
onto the floor and talked, asking questions about God, about
salvation, and about themselves as they studied their obviously
well-read Bibles.

They let me join them, camera and notebook in hand, one
Thursday night, and I longed to become a part of them as they
asked God for guidance and sought to learn how He affected their
day-to-day living. They were not preached to or taught the doctrines of any particular church. Theirs was an independent Bible

study, and their leader was determined it would remain ecumenical.

"This isn't a cult," the leader said as we watched forty soggy teens race through the rain. "We don't teach any weird doctrines; there are no gray areas of controversy."

The leader, a former member of a professional baseball team, was then assistant football and baseball coach at the high school. His tall figure became a familiar sight as he led his teams in prayer before each game. It was a new experience for many, but they didn't laugh. "Our biggest challenge is to help kids get their priorities straight, not just here and now, but for eternity," he said.

Class discussion topics in the past had included love, marriage, sex, the occult, and prayer. "We can schedule discussion on any doctrine anyone wants to know about," the leader said.

It was a happy place, that old country store, but it was also one of care and concern. On the night I was with them, their prayers focused on the man who owned the building, their friend and ally, George, who had cancer. "Anyone who wants to make a tape to send to George can meet at my locker tomorrow noon," a girl said. "I'll bring my recorder."

And their interest included people outside their circle. "I don't know who the dude was," a boy said, "but he fell into a vat of wax during a fire in a candle factory last week. He needs our prayers."

They re-read portions of Romans, Galatians, John, Mark, and Isaiah, and they prayed for George, for the man who fell in the wax, and for an ailing cousin. It was a time in which bumper stickers were proclaiming the death of God, but these students were proving God was indeed alive and well in our valley.

There never was any doubt of God's viability as far as one couple was concerned. Recently retired from their general store, they were free to travel and they chose to do it for God. "We didn't want to sit and rust out. We wanted to work for the Lord," they said between unpaid trips with an evangelistic team.

A secretary flew to Israel and then to Ireland with another evangelistic team. "Almost 50 people came forward for Christ during our crusade in Jerusalem and another 120 were baptized in the Jordan River," she said proudly.

But the best part of the trip was helping Irish children make tissue flowers and write letters to God. "It sounds so simple," she said, "but actually it was part of a miracle."

"Tissue flowers are a miracle?" I asked, thinking of the millions used every year to decorate floats at local festivals.

"We'd planned to use film strips and tapes we had shipped from home. But they got lost and didn't arrive until we were ready to leave. The only way we could work with the children was by buying materials from a local variety store. God intended it that way. We were supposed to be showing the people how they could conduct similar programs. By having to use what they could purchase readily, we accomplished our purpose. If we had used our material, they would have said, 'We can't do that.' God gave us a small miracle by not allowing the tapes to get there."

She had watched sniper fire and undergone daily searches for bombs and weapons, but she had returned with renewed faith, buoyed in part by the memory of a thousand people holding hands as they sang the Lord's Prayer at the close of the Irish crusade. "But don't give me any glory for it," she warned as she watched me take notes. "The glory belongs to the Lord."

Her mission took her to Ireland and Israel, but another couple had answered God's call to serve right here in the heart of the Bible Belt, and their mission, while not interspersed with rifle fire and weapons searches, was no less perilous.

Missionaries to rural Indiana, their mission is a tiny interdenominational church with no recorded membership.

"I didn't know we had local missionaries," I said. "I thought all missionaries went to India and Africa to convert people to Christianity. Most of the people in this area are Christians now. Some of them have different degrees of faith, but they are already Christian." I hated to come right out and ask them what they did, but my question was soon answered.

"When a rural church closes to merge with one in town, many of the people go where their denomination is, but the old church in the country could still hold small congregations, and that is where our group comes in," they replied.

"Our ministry's purpose is to bring back something alive and real where an individual can see another struggling with the conflict between his personal faith and the life he has to live."

Struggling with the conflict between his personal faith and the life he has to live. The words had a nice ring, but I was still years from understanding what they meant to me.

The list of Bible Belt Bushwhackers was almost as long as the list of crafts people. Some conducted Bible classes in their home, others became lay speakers, and still others turned their lives around because of God. Faith as practiced by these guerrilla fighters for the Lord gave new meaning to Galatians 2:20: "I have been crucified with Christ; it is no longer I who live, but Christ who lives in me; and the life I now live in the flesh I live by faith in the Son of God, who loved me and gave himself for me."

The God who loved me and gave himself for me. How that God must have cringed at his closet disciple who had become a church dropout because someone had differed with her and had gone so far as to pray for her. It was a sobering realization, and a time for self-reflection, of goals met and not met, of answered prayers that sometimes seemed to reflect St. Theresa of Avila's philosophy: "More tears are shed over answered prayers than Heaven forgot."

I knew my life would never be the same after I'd interviewed the Bible Belt Bushwhackers, and I was still groping with stubborn pride when my sons, reared on Sunday school and church services, began attending church again. "You really should go too," they said.

I let the challenge taunt me as I continued to sleep late on Sundays, even as I learned I could write articles that would sell to national publications during the time I should be in church. "God wants me to use this time to pull myself together, to get prepared for a new week on the paper," I told myself, but I knew I was rationalizing. It took several false starts, attempts at worship that left me feeling unfulfilled and frustrated. There was something there I wanted, but I couldn't let go of my pride long enough to reach for.

Before long, however, I was again part of the congregation at the familiar brick church on the corner. No one said they missed me when I left, and no one rushed to welcome me when I returned. I had simply come home, and we all knew it was better that nothing was said.

It was while I was still enjoying the glow of renewed fellowship that Todd issued the most provocative challenge of all: "You really should become a Christian writer."

"I am a writer, and I am a Christian," I remarked.

"It's not the same. You should become a Christian writer," he said.

15

Indecisively Yours

"**F**lying with one arm is easy once you get the feel of it," a handicapped pilot had said. And so, I imagined, was hanging once you were dead. Becoming a Christian writer sounded almost that difficult.

Todd's suggestion made sense; in fact, it was an area I longed to enter but feared to tread for fear lack of Biblical knowledge would expose me as a closet Christian who should have stayed in the closet a little longer to study.

And I knew, too, we had failed if our paper were to be judged according to proper journalistic criteria. While I became impatient with those who hinted bad news should be censored, it pleased me when a reader said, "That's the kind of article I like," after a feature appeared about someone's ministry or lapidary work. They were "good news" stories for a "good news" newspaper.

"Life isn't always a bowl of cherries," Polly would scoff. "You should show the wormy apples, too."

Of course there were wormy apples. No community is without them. Objective writing was virtually impossible when a teenager was beaten so savagely by two of his peers that he died—strangled on his own vomit. "Involuntary manslaughter," the judge ruled. "Asphyxiation was the cause of death, not the blows." No matter that the boy's head was covered with lumps and no amount of makeup could conceal the swelling in his neck

149

as he was buried by his weeping classmates and heartbroken family. Within five weeks his assailants were out of jail, boasting. No written word could express the outrage we felt, that the community felt.

But what of the other omissions in my writing?

In protecting my own family, I had shut off avenues of communication that would have been helpful to our readers and to the very people I tried to protect. I had hidden our involvement with the occult and covered up our failure at do-it-yourself Christianity. Much had been swept under an editorial rug.

Being a Christian writer did not mean seeing only the good side of life. Christ didn't need any indecisive disciples. "If I ever wrote a book, it would have to be titled 'Indecisively Yours,' " I told Todd.

"You don't seem to have any trouble deciding when I should go to bed," he reminded me.

"That's not what I mean," I growled. "I mean like even trying to figure out what's right and what's wrong. Like knowing what to do with an answered prayer."

"God answers prayers."

"I know that. That's just the trouble. He answered my prayer for a paper of my own with not one but two papers. And He's never let us down, never. We've never missed an issue. We've managed to publish a paper regardless of appendectomies, babies, or tornadoes. There have been Thursdays I'm sure God pushed the car to get it through the drifts to the printer. I can't even count the times when we were the last people down our road before it drifted completely closed."

"You forgot about the time the semi hit you on the way to the printer," he said.

"We made it home with the paper intact, didn't we?"

"What are you trying to say?"

"I'm saying that God has answered my prayers abundantly. He gave us a weekly newspaper. He's helped us keep it. But the truth is, I no longer like it. Your father hates it."

"I thought he always wanted a business of his own."

"He did. He still does. But he doesn't want a newspaper. He's discovered he likes printing; in fact he loves it. But writing isn't for him. He doesn't like to sell advertising, he doesn't like sports, and he doesn't like to take pictures."

"How about you?"

"There's a lot I like, but there's a lot I dislike. I like creating advertising layouts, but I hate to sell them. I like to interview people, but I can't stand chasing up and down football fields."

"Why don't you sell the paper?"

"I prayed for that paper and God answered my prayers. It wouldn't be right to tell Him I've changed my mind."

"You could become a Christian writer."

"I could learn to fly, too, if I had wings."

"Suit yourself."

It was time for an editorial conference. Loren and I lingered late over tea and coffee and discussed the problem. It was a lumpy one. Both of us believed with all our hearts that we would have failed years ago had it not been for God. He had buoyed us when we were too tired to move, when complaints outweighed compliments ten to one, and through gunfire, illness, and death. When finances hit rock bottom, a check from a slow customer appeared. When we needed extra help, it had been there. God had been with us always, and on Thursdays He had really looked after us.

We added our lists of debits and credits, much as I had done in my banking days.

On the plus side, we had an answered prayer. The discipline required for meeting deadlines had taught me to write at odd times, the condition of the refrigerator and living room windows notwithstanding. Spin-offs from several of the centerfolds had found their way to other magazines.

On the negative side, I had a husband I loved who had come to view my answered prayer as the devil's payment of a debt owed. He had tried to learn to like it, but it was like trying to enjoy spinach when you can't stand the sight or smell of it.

"Is there anything about the business you like?" I asked, knowing the answer without having to hear his reply.

"Job printing," he said, his eyes sparkling with enthusiasm. "I love it."

"And here's the job department," the former owner told us as we surveyed for the first time the world of Linotypes, presses, turtles, and quoins. We paid it little attention, concentrating, instead, on an inky world in which we had no experience. Over the years we had learned the job department is not exactly a stepchild in newspaper offices because it often has to provide the backbone of the business, the income needed to support the paper. But it certainly was not an important part of our decision to buy the *News*. It was something that came with it, something with which to fill Fridays after the paper was printed and mailed on Thursday. It represented a world of letterheads, envelopes, and business forms I liked to use but had no desire to help create.

"Do you want to sell the *News?*" I asked.

"More than anything," Loren replied, "but that decision has to be yours. I know how much you wanted it, and I'm not going to be the one to say it has to go. That has to come from you. My feelings shouldn't enter into it."

"God answered our prayers. . . ."

"Your prayers, remember. I just thank Him instead of going around asking for things."

"Both our prayers," I corrected. "Besides, we tried to sell the paper once."

"We were just discouraged then."

"And now?"

"This is different."

Remembering Hattie's sign, I said, "God doesn't like quitters."

"I doubt if he likes us the way we are, especially on Thursday. We get awfully tired and crabby."

"He's kept us going. He'll keep us going. He won't let us down."

"Do you think He could speed up the help a little?" he asked.

He was joking, but his blue eyes drained gray said help was needed.

Within weeks, we both became quitters, giving up our only hobbies and becoming living proof that every person needs some outlet besides his or her work. Flying went first. There simply was not enough time. It seemed unfair to create miniature room settings while my husband worked through the night, and I put into storage all the miniatures I'd hoarded over the years. Instead, I wrote more articles, setting new deadlines for myself, deadlines that knotted my nervous system and caused my back and neck to throb constantly.

Finally, there came a day I could no longer bottle up the frustration I felt, and I invited Marilyn Kruger for tea. The first of my centerfold interviews, she was also the first to mention her relationship with God, a litany I was to hear from nearly everyone I interviewed. There is no question in my mind that God had a purpose in sending me out camera in hand to see what others were doing. It was the greatest training any journalist could have.

Marilyn and I had discovered we were kindred spirits. She was and is a friend with whom Romans 12:15 comes alive: "Rejoice with those who rejoice, weep with those who weep." We talked and talked and wept together, groping for the right words, yet not caring either.

"Have you ever fully surrendered your life to Christ, really accepted Him?" she asked.

"I am a Christian," I said. "I was baptized years ago." The words sounded faintly familiar, much like the statement I had made to Todd, "I am a writer. I am a Christian." "But it's not the same," he had said, and now it was Marilyn's turn.

"You went through the motions," she said, "but have you ever really fully accepted Him? Have you ever really let go your hold on your life and let Jesus take over? Have you ever really put your primary trust in God?"

"I have trusted God's leading with my heart and soul," I said.

No words were ever truer. But even as I spoke, I knew in my heart I had never fully accepted Jesus, had in fact turned away from His admonition, "I am the way, the truth and life: no man comes to the Father but by me." But I had tried. I had found it difficult to understand much of what I read about the man called Jesus. While I had never fully subscribed to the existentialist belief that man is totally free and responsible for his acts, I had maintained a certain freedom of my own even as I had developed a strong reliance on God's help. I had sought His help in every move I made, but I had been confused by His son. The Immaculate Conception was alien to my realistic viewpoint, but I think the one part of the New Testament that really confused me was the story about Jesus withering a fig tree for not bearing fruit before the season. It sounded like a temper tantrum, and as a mother trying to train her sons to remain calm when things went wrong, I was repulsed. Still, temper tantrum or not, I also felt His death for *us* was the waste of a perfectly good life.

Yet I had accepted Christ into my life when I was baptized at an age far older than most children and had been accepted into full church membership along with my parents and brother. But I still had reservations about this man who withered fig trees even as I knew in my heart He was the answer to my problems.

"He can help," Marilyn said. "He will help."

For months after Marilyn's visit, I prayed for God's help, often in the driver's seat of my six-cylinder car as I waited for it to warm up for another busy day. "I want to see Jesus, to feel His presence," I had told Marilyn.

"It sounds like you want the Second Coming more than wanting Him to enter your life," she had said. Her words hit a sore spot—the one centered between my shoulder blades—and I had retreated even more snugly into my spiritual closet.

But finally the day came when I knew I could no longer control my life, even as I had always known I could not live it without God's help. I climbed into my spiritual closet, that bright red car everyone knew so well, closed the door, started the engine, and told God I could no longer handle my life, that it had become too complex for me to manage. "Take it to use however you can," I prayed.

I had read about people who turned their lives over to God, and I had talked to many who said they felt nothing right away, but that they had known God had heard. I expected this same nothing, but, instead, I felt a glow, a realization that in fully yielding to God, I had fully accepted Christ—and His death. And I came to understand the fact that Christ had withered me as surely as He had withered the fig tree. He had forced my old self to die that I might enter into His life for myself.

The closet Christian who retreated to her car for prayer was out of the closet, fully accepting Christ and His teachings in her life. It was a giant step, and I rejoiced, even as I continued to race from meeting to meeting, from deadline to deadline.

God had answered my prayer with the greatest gift of all, my full acceptance of His Son, but the answer to another of my prayers still held us tightly in its grip. Advertising sales continued to make me ill, and sports still had no appeal. Loren continued to work around the clock, although his outlook and the boys' lives changed with my complete acceptance of Christ. They had already fully accepted Him. I had become a millstone for them as I sought signs and waited for His presence and touch. I rejoiced at their patience, but I knew, too, that my answered prayer was strangling them. Had there been another man in my life, they could not have resented him any more than they resented the *News*.

"Troubles?" Polly asked as we met on the street in the midst of my pursuit of advertising.

"Does it show?"

"Every move you make says, 'Here is an unhappy person,' " she said. Still outspoken as ever, this was a vastly different Polly than the one who with Willy had boasted "a Wright is always right," even as we had known nothing was really right with them. Willy had drawn comfort from sports cars and other

women. Polly had had an affair with her boss. Their dalliances
and our schedules had caused rifts in our friendship, and we had
seen them little over the past few years. But something had
happened to them in recent months, and both had become warm-
er, more lovable. Polly had quit her job and was now actively
doing volunteer work in the community. She had stopped to help
with the mailing a few times, and we had marveled at the change
in her. The bitter Polly was gone, replaced by a warm, loving
Polly, a Polly who clearly adored her husband. And Willy, when
he stopped by to see how she was doing, no longer wore his usual
lean, hungry look. He, too, had changed.

"What happened?" I asked Polly one day as she rode with me
to the printer.

"Christ came into our lives," she said. She didn't elaborate or
lecture. It was a simple statement of faith, one so strong I wished
God had made me a cheerleader instead of a popcorn popper in
the ball game of life. I wanted to hug her and shout, but, instead,
I blinked back tears of joy and drove on as I whispered thanks to
God. So many of our old friends were gone. In the midst of our
own pursuit of ink and deadlines, we had seen the painful demise
of Ruby and Jim's store, had seen Marty and Russ close their real
estate office, and we still grieved at Nancy's death and the route
Paul's life had taken since. The group that once gathered to
discuss books and later to talk to Ouija had scattered with the
wind. Of all of them, Polly had seemed the least likely candidate
as a confidant, yet I found myself pouring out my misery to her.

"Have you ever fully surrendered your life to Christ, really
accepted Him?"

It was the same question Marilyn had asked months earlier,
except this time I could wholeheartedly say, "Yes."

"Have you ever really let go of your hold on your life and let
God take over?"

"He answered our—my—prayer for the *News*."

"Did He? Or did you try to mastermind Him?"

"Me mastermind God?"

"Don't act so surprised. You know what I mean. Did you take over?"

"I might have, I suppose. Loren says I'm getting a real take-charge kind of attitude, and I guess he's right. I used to hate it when Marty bristled up whenever anyone said anything about Russ or the real estate business, but if someone gives Loren a rough time or says anything against the *News* or the 'News Media,' I get furious, ready to go to battle."

"Were you ready to go to battle to get the *News?*"

"I wanted it."

"Why?"

"You know why. You were at that meeting when I announced my life's dream was to own the *News*. I wanted to learn to write. Loren wanted a business of his own."

"Then your prayer has been answered."

"The paper was an answer to all my prayers."

"Wrong."

I stared at her, uncomprehending. The paper *had* been an answer to all my prayers. I had learned to write. Loren had learned a profession he loved. Who could not say our prayers had been answered? The paper was the fulfillment of every dream, every prayer I had had since I first felt the thrill of pen and ink, paper and pencil, had first experienced the joy of the printed word. It had replaced camel-back journalism. It had . . . My thoughts trailed off as I heard Polly's words, "The paper answered your prayer, but you didn't need it. You didn't need it then and you don't need it now."

"I don't know if I needed it, but I certainly wanted it. A rose blooms where it is planted. I was planted here. The paper was the answer." Even as I sputtered my response, I knew the words sounded feeble. Had I substituted one fantasy for another? Had the stereotype of the crusading editor replaced my youthful visions of camel caravans?

"It sounds exciting, really," Polly was saying. "Is it?"

"It can be," I said slowly. "Fantastically exciting. I love the people I meet, I like writing about the good things they do. I know you've been disappointed that I didn't tackle abortion or child abuse in the paper, but I've really enjoyed being a 'good news' reporter."

"It's not as important that you didn't write about those things as it is that you can't come out with a big 'But' I'm hearing but you aren't saying."

I wished I could feel as positive about everything as Polly did. Her conversion had been dramatic, and she seemed so full of answers. My own conversion had been slow and painful and even as I rejoiced in my newfound relationship with Jesus, I knew in my heart all was not well in my life.

"Were you in love with a stereotype?" she asked.

"Cluttered desks, clattering presses, beat-up typewriters," I added. "The kind of editor who crusades for justice, who exposes political corruption—all kinds of exciting things." *Things* sounded weak, insufficient, much like my reasons for wanting to own a newspaper were beginning to seem.

"I seem to recall seeing you take pictures of a riot. Your editorials about the school system won awards. You've gone to bat for children with learning defects, and that article about the man who is now alive and well because the EMTs were able to sustain life with CPR was a tear-jerker."

"That one was fun. I enjoyed it. But the others cost me trips to the doctor. It's one thing to picture yourself as a crusader and quite another to have to fill a role that makes you sick." Even as I talked, I could see and hear a camel caravan fade into the distance. My dream had become distorted, ink-stained, and filled with pain.

"Have you told God about any of these problems?"

"I think He can see them without my crying on His shoulder. Besides, I owe Him. He answered my prayers."

"The paper was what you substituted," she said sharply. "It answered your prayer, but you didn't need it. You didn't need it then and you don't need it now."

It was the second time in the past five minutes she had said that. It sounded blasphemous. We *had* needed it. God had answered my prayer for it. A kind and loving Father would not provide something His children didn't need.

"God has a lot of help to offer," she said.

"He's supplied all our needs. You wouldn't believe the times He's bailed us out."

"And evidently you don't believe how much He has to offer. He's a good listener. Talk to Him again."

"I'll try," I promised, but I faltered. Where my friends had burned their Ouija boards without hesitation while I continued to cling to my spiritualist books, I clung now to my indecisiveness. I turned back to the Bible, and the truth slowly hit me. What I had feared most about Christ's words and actions was His decisiveness. He knew what was right, what His Father would have Him do. I tended to falter and stumble, and in my gratitude for answered prayer I had really cut myself loose, making myself responsible for my acts once that prayer had been answered. I turned again to the works of Soren Kierkegaard, one of the existentialists I had studied during my brief return to college, and read, *Prayer does not change God but changes him who prays.*

"Does not change God but changes him who prays," I repeated, shuddering to think how much the quiet woman who seldom raised her voice had changed over the years, how the once calm woman was now given to anger, tears, and frustration. God had answered prayer, but I had changed, and the change had not been good.

God had accepted me when I surrendered my life to Him, had given me the gift of His only Son, a gift that I could never earn. Now I had to come to Him with a prayer of relinquishment. The take-charge, now-hear-this, this-is-how-I-want-it-to-be prayer was replaced with one in which I again asked Him to take over my life and in which I admitted I'd pretty well messed it up. I thanked Him again for His Son, whom I now accepted as my Savior. "And," I whispered, "if it be Thy will, help us sell the paper."

It was a big step, and I gulped as I said the words. I was asking

God to take back His answered prayer. It wasn't until later that I realized I had passed the decision to Him in a prayer so indecisive I might as well have said "indecisively yours" instead of amen.

16

Someone Has to Pop the Corn

No temptation has overtaken you that is not common to man. God is faithful, and he will not let you be tempted beyond your strength, but with the temptation will also provide the way of escape, that you may be able to endure it.

These words from 1 Corinthians were tacked to the bulletin board over my desk, and I read them every day, drawing strength from them as I waited for the telephone to ring and for the evening mail to arrive. The *News* had officially been listed for sale for over a year, but the prospects of its being sold within the next ten years seemed remote.

Have no anxiety about anything, but in everything by prayer and supplication with thanksgiving let your requests be made known to God. And the peace of God, which passes all understanding, will keep your hearts and your minds in Christ Jesus. These words of Paul's were also tacked to the bulletin board, and I read and reread them. They gave me hope as I continued to pray, "If it be Thy will, let us sell the paper."

We assumed it was not God's will that the *News* be sold when more than twenty people drove from as far as Florida and Missouri to examine the prospects and found them lacking.

I had wanted to own a weekly newspaper because I wanted to learn to write, and it had proven a relentless teacher. Much of the writing had been rewarding, none more fun than my personal column, *Odds and Ends,* in which I poked fun at myself, my husband, and our sons without trying to make anyone seem the "heavy." Written at odd intervals often determined by who was sick or when there was enough space, the clippings filled a loose leaf notebook. "You should put them together in a book," friends persisted. I gave the thought about as much consideration as I had Todd's suggestion, "You should become a Christian writer."

I looked at the columns again. I laughed at some and cried over others. "They've been fun," I told God. "Thank You." The strain of the day was heavy on me, and I wearily confided, "I'm not sure newspapering is the kind of writing I want to do. Please direct me in the way You want me to go." I had cut the first apron string.

Some people hear the voice of God speak to them. Others define it as a still, small voice. In my case, I awoke with a book outline racing through my mind, begging to be compiled. It had already been written. It just needed arranging.

My work load did not slacken because of the book. The newspaper still had to be written, edited, pasted-up, delivered to the printer, and mailed. Advertising had to be sold, and the bookkeeping had to be done. And keeping a family of four in clean socks and underwear is no easier than trying to keep a nine-room house clean, but I did them all while I somehow made time to get together a collection of columns that fell into some semblance of order after several false starts. The packet looked impressive when I dropped my query and sample chapters into the mail slot and set off to sell advertising.

Months later, I received a letter from an editorial assistant. "We like the material, but we would like to see it rewritten using more of a Christian witness," she said.

"They want more," I told Loren, tears of joy streaming down my face.

"Will you have any trouble rewriting it?"

"It'll be fun."

"You have my wholehearted support."

"Thanks," I said, blowing him a kiss. And then I cried for

three days. I was in a state of terror. "Why me? Did God, like Todd, want me to be a Christian writer?" I'll have to write and tell them I can't do it, I'd tell myself. One minute later I'd be convinced I could do it. In the end, I turned it over to God.

"If You want me to do it, will You help?"

He must have wanted me to do it, because my tears dried, reason prevailed, and a special issue for basketball notwithstanding, the book was written, often late at night and sometimes at the office when I should have been working on something for the paper. But it was written. There were times I felt I was only God's typist, that He was dictating words to me, and I feared I would blunder, that I would misunderstand His message. No writing has ever been more fun, more rewarding than that. It caused me to reexamine my own beliefs, thoughts, and actions.

The result was *Born Again . . . but still wet behind the ears,* and it was so much fun, I decided to use a Christian witness approach in the columns I wrote for the *News.* Our church was then involved in special Lenten services, and I had joined prayer study and sermon preparation groups that were giving new depth to my limited Christian experience. They also provided the basis for two columns.

Odds and Ends, while certainly not sacrilegious, had always been strictly family. The two columns would be a contradiction of all that had preceded them, and I worried how they would be accepted. The results put my fears to rest. They proved to be the most popular of any I had written, prompting readers to call, write, and drop in to tell me they had enjoyed them, had shared them with friends.

"At last," I boasted to God, "I'm coming out of my closet. I can be decisive about something. I'm not afraid for people to know I'm a Christian. I won't be upset by other people any more. I've got it all figured out now."

If I had talked on a party line with the devil himself listening to every word, I could not have imagined the series of events to follow, situations that would cause me to reevaluate everything I believed in, past prejudices and mistakes, strengths and weaknesses. They gave me a startling reminder of the validity of Matthew 23:12: "Whoever exalts himself will be humbled." Or of 1 Corinthians 8:2: "If anyone imagines that he knows something, he does not yet know as he ought to know." Oh, did I have a lot to learn.

My boast was still hanging in the air when Loren called to report there had been a bad accident. "I think Willy Wright's dead."

"Oh no!" I cried. "Why now?" Polly had become my friend, my confidant, my spiritual sounding board. With Marilyn, she formed the nucleus of my growing Christian fellowship. Once the antagonist in my life, she had become a mentor. She and Willy had grown since Christ entered their lives. They had so much to offer. Willy had begun teaching Sunday school and Polly was working with underprivileged children. Together they had formed a Bible study class that drew together more than a dozen church drop-outs now well on their way to rejoining their own churches. They planned other classes, and Willy was seriously considering going back to college to get a degree in counseling and guidance. "But I have to be selective," he said. "The school must put an emphasis on Christian faith. I can't live without Christ, and I can't counsel anyone any other way. Christ has to be the foundation."

Now Willy was dead, a traffic fatality according to statistics, but in our small area his death would be felt on a more personal basis, would in fact be the turning point in many lives.

Willy had died instantly of a broken neck sustained in a head-on crash with a drunken driver. "I told you drinking was no good for anyone," Hattie Hooper told everyone who would listen, and we all nodded our agreement, even Paul Carter, too drunk to fully understand what she was saying.

A sorrowing community drew together to lay Willis Wright to rest. "He was a good man," the minister said, emphasizing an opinion we had only recently formed ourselves. Willy Wright had been a good man. He had loved Polly and their son Wee Willy, he had led the fight for one high school long before that was a popular opinion, and his had become an active voice in the church and in the community. Now that voice had been silenced by a man seldom sober long enough to tie his own shoelaces.

Suddenly a gasp interrupted the eulogy, and everyone turned to stare in the direction of the Sandlers. Norman P. was slumped in his pew; Patience and Sonny were trying to fan him, and the people around him were attempting to loosen his tie, arguing whether to try to get him on his feet or to have him lie down. Two members of the crowd, recently trained as emergency medical technicians, rushed to him and began administering CPR.

Willy's funeral continued after the men left in the ambulance with Norman P., and I found myself alternately praying for Polly and for Norman P. There had been times when I could not in my wildest imaginings have foreseen the day I would pray for either, but now all I could do was weep for them both, one newly widowed and the other overcome by grief.

No one who had seen Norman P. slump in his pew was surprised to learn he had been dead on arrival at the hospital. Norman P. Sandler, long our foe, long the foe of Ruby and Jim Pearl, long the foe of anyone who stood in his way or who threatened his corner of publicity, had gone out the way he lived, in the most public manner anyone could imagine.

I remembered Norman P. over the years. The pious Norman who needed only a halo to make him an angel before men. The stormin' Norman who vented his rage when we printed stories of Sonny's drunken driving escapades and divorces. The Sunday Christian Norman who violated his contract with Ruby and Jim. The publicity seeking Norman who called on radio stations and founded shoppers and newspapers at will, but who never had anything for the local newspaper because "no one reads it." The fuming Norman who obviously read the paper and found it lacking. But there also was the loving Norman who clearly adored

Patience and Sonny. And the concerned Norman who called daily after Todd's leg was broken, who sent flowers in appreciation of an article he'd enjoyed in the paper "nobody reads." There had been many Norman P. Sandlers, and we doubted we had even begun to know them all. Now they were all dead, and the community had lost a vital element, a voice, however strident, that really had loved *our* town until it had been silenced.

When Joy died, I wrote, "No one has yet printed a handbook to tell editors how to write obituaries of friends and relatives. Until they do, all we can say is, "Good bye. We loved you." How I wished there was such a handbook when I found myself writing the obituaries of my father-in-law, of a friend so young and vital as Nancy Carter, of one as old and valued as Sophie Palmer. And how I yearned for such a handbook now as I wrote the obituaries of a man I had too long been alienated from and for another whom I had often disliked to the point of hatred. "Just give them the facts, Ann," I admonished myself as I sat at the typewriter and viewed the blank sheet of paper through a veil of tears. Writing obituaries is considered beginner's work on most metropolitan newspapers, but maybe it's easier when the name is one of hundreds, not one you have laughed with, cried with, or even fought with.

But if writing the obituaries was hard, writing the court news that followed Willy Wright's death was even more difficult. The judge found the drunken driver guilty on only one charge—driving left of center.

"What kind of justice is that?" I raged to Loren. "Willy was perfectly innocent. The other man was intoxicated. Willy is dead and his killer is scot free. Polly is a widow. Wee Willy is half-orphaned and all that judge can do is fine that miserable drunkard twenty-five dollars for driving left of center." It was impossible to report just the facts without getting on an editorial soapbox. I knew why justice was always blindfolded. It couldn't see. Was this the fury Jesus felt with the moneychangers? Or was it mine?

But the ink had barely dried on the court news before another grinding crash left a second left-of-center fatality. Dead was a man on a motorcycle, a man no one in the community knew, a man riding on his own side of the road but killed by a car that veered across the center line. The driver was Silas Monroe. Silas, the man who warned we would either become religious fanatics or alcoholics, a man who had long ago turned his life over to God, a good man by anyone's standards, a man who worked hard in church, a lay speaker much in demand. Silas had given employment to more marginal workers than anyone would ever know. Everyone liked Silas Monroe; he was everyone's father and big brother rolled into one. Now Silas Monroe had killed a man by swerving the wrong direction to avoid a head-on crash.

But when Silas' day in court came, he didn't receive a twenty-five dollar fine for driving left of center. Instead, he was found guilty of involuntary manslaughter and given a jail sentence. Hell hath no fury like the wrath Silas' sentence evoked. "Where's an ounce of justice in that sentence?" I asked. "Tell me why a good church worker gets a stiffer sentence than a drunk. Tell me." No one could. "For the wrongdoer will be paid back for the wrong he has done, and there is no partiality," I read in Colossians 3:25. But wasn't the drunken driver who killed Willy Wright also wrong? Why was he free while Silas was going to jail? Why was the judge showing partiality?

It was a question I could have asked myself. Instead, I wept for Silas and prayed for him, indecisively formulating plans for helping him I knew I could never fulfill. I was still passing my own judgment on the judicial system when a minister came in with his church news. "What are members of your church going to do for Silas?" he asked.

"We're all praying for him," I answered.

"That's not enough," he said. "You should offer to do something. Some of us ministers are going to get together and see if we can go to jail for him or even with him. We can't let him face this alone."

"If the area ministers do that, the least the members of his church could do would be to go with him or serve in his place," I said.

As soon as he left to call his pastor friends, I dialed my prayer partner, Agatha, Silas' oldest daughter. "Let's go to jail for your dad," I said in a breathless whisper that fairly burst with pride that I was actually making the suggestion.

"Oh, Ann, that would be just terrible," she said.

"What's so terrible about wanting to help him? He got a bad decision."

"He doesn't think so. He was driving left of center, even if he did think he could swerve out of the cycle's path. He was where he should not have been, and he fully accepts the fact that the accident was his fault. He absolutely wants to serve the sentence himself. He'd feel like he cheated God if someone served it for him."

"But your father's a good man; he only swerved to get out of the other man's way, to make room for the cycle to turn."

"That doesn't alter his conviction that he is guilty. He feels he has to take the punishment himself."

"But everyone thinks the punishment is unfair."

"Dad doesn't. He wants to serve the term himself."

Her words had a ring of finality, and I hung up, dejected that I wouldn't be going to jail, yet a bit curious about how I could make such a definite judgment about the guilt or innocence of two men. Did I determine it by the fact that one drank heavily and the other was a lay leader? Not very good criteria for any judgment. "Thank God, I'm not the final judge," I whispered in a statement that was both prayer and a sigh of relief. At the same time, I felt a bit of self-pride: I'd had the courage to make a suggestion.

The telephone rang before I had moved my hand from it, and my sense of pride exploded into a million tiny pieces when I heard the caller's voice. *Claiming to be wise, they became fools.* Paul's words from Romans 1:22 echoed through my mind. Would I never learn to quit boasting? I might be out of the closet, but God certainly wasn't finished with me yet. I had—and still have—much to learn about humility.

The caller was the local tavern owner, and he had an advertisement he was bringing over. "Come ahead," I said weakly, my good "vibes" giving way to apprehension. It had been more than a dozen years since we had run any liquor advertisements, and the wounds generated by those agency "house" ads had only begun to heal. The advertisement that was coming would be far more blatant than the earlier ones had ever been. I could only wonder at the changes that had been made in the community's attitude toward liquor during those years.

But there had been changes at the state level, and in the previous session of the legislature, liquor retailers had worked hard to win the right to advertise prices. The legislation had resulted in large ads in metropolitan papers, but we had never solicited liquor advertising and didn't feel we would be affected by it. We had canceled the old national liquor ad years ago, and the churches had ceased praying for us, had indeed given us a backbone of news about their activities.

Now a liquor ad was coming, and I could not find it in my conscience to tell the man no, however much I might dislike his product, however many prayers I might be whispering that all would go well when the ad was printed.

The tavern owner wanted the type large and the ad placed on the back page. "We will if there is room," I said, "but I can't promise you anything."

"You look at the front page and then turn to the back page," Jim Pearl always said. Most advertisers agreed, but unless someone specified the back page, we tried to rotate the ads so everyone could have a chance at the "prime spot." Unfortunately, the liquor ad could be worked in with the others scheduled there. There would be no hiding it; it would be right there on the outside for the whole world or at least 2100 subscribers to see.

Four letters out of a possible twenty-one hundred cannot be

considered a landslide, but my own wavering indecision coupled with their vocalness, made me cringe as I opened each. "You shouldn't have printed that advertisement," Hattie Hooper wrote. "Why didn't you stop and consider Proverbs 22:3: 'A prudent man sees danger and hides himself; but the simple go on, and suffer for it?'"

Not convinced I had read her letter, Hattie came to call in person, shaking her head as she marched into my office. "Such a shame, and just when our Ann was becoming a Christian writer."

My stomach ached, knotted, and twisted. Never, when I became a Christian, did I promise not to advertise a liquor store. I knew many Christians who drank without going to excess . . . but . . . Always that big but. But, what?

I had been talked out of going to jail for my friend and into running an advertisment I didn't really want. I knew that some of my charismatic friends would say the devil had won a big victory. I hated to credit him with anything right then, but I knew indecisiveness had won another round if no one or no other thing had.

"I had no right to deny that man an ad," I kept telling myself, but when I picked up a trade publication the story that seemed to jump at me was about a metropolitan newspaper that had said it would no longer advertise pornographic movies. The decision would cost the paper $75,000 per year. Had I said no to the liquor ad, the decision would have reduced our income $11.20. Our total advertising revenue for the previous year had been less than half what the metropolitan publication would lose on pornography. I found myself whispering a silent prayer of thanks that our towns had no theaters, massage parlors, or race tracks. The indecisiveness would have killed me.

We had had almost fifteen years of being able to say, "I did it my way," and until I ceased being a closet Christian, I had been able to say, "I did it my way," with relish. Now I found myself torn between doing it my way and *His* way. Christ had poured wine at the wedding. Would he also have advertised the winemaker? I did not know. All I knew for certain was that Matthew

6:24 is right: "No one can serve two masters; for either he will hate the one and love the other, or he will be devoted to the one and despise the other. You cannot serve God and mammon." And I preferred Christ to advertising whiskey, good news to bad news, stories of stained glass craftsmanship to football, features about needlepoint and mushroom art to even considering writing about Polly's neighbor's abortion. Now I could understand for the first time what the rural missionary meant when he referred to the struggle between a man's personal faith and the life he has to live. I finally knew why God had sent me to the interviews for centerfold articles. It had been a growing experience He knew I needed.

But was I still an ostrich with its head stuck in the sand? A person content to go blissfully through life without really touching bases? Maybe. I'd told the school board during my quest for remedial programs that some people are just naturally slow learners. Now it seemed I'd really been talking about myself. It had taken me fifteen years of hard work to finally understand that God has need for all kinds of persons—advocates like Hattie Hooper, promoters like Norman P. Sandler, and cookie pushers like Sophie Palmer. He needs the kind of investigative reporters who broke the story of Watergate, the kind of writers who can cover football games well, who can attend Congressional hearings, who can mount camels and ride off in caravans. And He needs corn poppers. In the game of life, someone has to pop the corn, provide the fluff, report the quiet pursuits of fellow popcorn makers, the people creating their own little niches in the world, niches that will never make page one. And I was that kind of person. I much preferred writing the good news, adding the fluff to life, popping the corn, to selling advertising, reporting school board meetings or making decisions about liquor advertising. There would always be a touch more of fun-loving Sophie Palmer in me than advocate Hattie Hooper, but, thankfully, God has need for all of us.

Silas Monroe had said, "You'll either become religious fanatics or alcoholics," and we had become neither, but liquor had proved to be the catalyst in our growth as Christians. It had helped turn us from church members into frustrated do-it-yourself Christians, and now it had moved me to the moment of decision Loren had said would finally have to be mine.

The loving Father who watched us falter and fumble for fifteen years had been with us in sickness and health, had watched over us in our struggles with fire, ink, and deadlines. He knew we were working against ourselves, but He was patient as He answered all our prayers, not just one. It was a love and patience beyond comprehension, a love so great I finally knew it would permit one more prayer, the biggest, the most difficult and the most necessary prayer of all.

I turned again to God. Where once I surrendered my life to Him, I now let go of my hold on the *News*. "If it be Thy will that we sell the paper, help us find a buyer," was replaced by, "I was wrong. I goofed. Thank You for your help. We could not have made it without You, but now we have to say, 'We're ready to sell. *I* have to say I'm ready to sell.' " I wept as I whispered the words, but they had to be said. I had to relinquish my life's dream, my answered prayer. And it hurt.

But in two weeks the *News* was sold. The new owners had no desire for the job department that had become Loren's pride and joy, and he found himself with computers, darkrooms, and presses—everything he needed to launch a new business.

The same day we signed the contract, a bank called and offered me a job. It had taken me almost fifteen years to realize the answer I prayed for was not the answer to my prayers, but I was disappointed. Surely, someone would offer me a writing job that didn't involve late meetings and that wouldn't wrack me with indecision. Had my painful apprenticeship been for nothing, the awards merely morale boosters?

Tearfully, I turned again to God. "Is this what You want for me?"

If ever I heard the voice of God, it was that night. "Trust Me." The message was loud and clear—inaudible—but so distinct I could no longer doubt God had a plan for me, that He would not fail me even if He put me on "hold" with only Thursdays free to write. (Thursday is traditionally the bank's day to be closed, just as it was fifteen years earlier when my day off coincided with our publication day.)

A night or two later, I slipped on wet leaves and smashed my knee. I was back where I had been fifteen years before—working for a bank—and back where I'd been one paper later—with a bloody knee and torn hose. The fall seemed to roll back the years as if they had never existed.

"It's easy to see this is where we came in," I wrote in my final column. "I'll miss newspapering, but it is without regret that I write 'The End.' "

It took me fifteen years to understand that God does not close doors but simply creates detours, and to realize that He would not consider me a drop-out if I asked Him to take back an answered prayer.

Now an officer of the same bank in which I worked right after high school, my job has evolved from part-time teller to head teller to marketing director. It has taken me to school in Colorado and to more seminars than I can count. I have undertaken an entirely new communications role, one that permits me to add fluff to other people's lives in the form of children's savings programs, incentives and, yes, even popcorn. At the same time, it lets me work with people, helping them plan the savings program best suited for them, showing them banking can be fun, too. It's a different type of writing, of serving, than I had in mind when I dreamed of camel caravans and, because of stringent federal regulations regarding banking, it is far more technical than any of the centerfolds or *Odds and Ends.* But there's always Thursday for those things. I'll always be part popcorn maker, and Thursdays, evenings, and the pre-dawn hours before I head to the bank give me time for that kind of writing. Without the fifteen years of training God permitted us, I never would have learned the discipline to handle these dual roles—make that triple because we still have piles of dirty clothes to wash and a lot of dust to move each week. Had it not been for Him, I would still be dreaming of someday owning a newspaper and would be the ever-present person at any gathering who says, "I would write if I had the time."

The job department that came to mean so much to Loren has been expanded into a full-fledged business located in a bright, new building on a quiet street in the town we love as much today as we did eighteen years ago. Make that towns. We have no reservations in saying the two towns that comprised the *News* beat are the greatest to be found anywhere. The tree-lined streets now wend their way past businesses owned by people who had never heard of the area eighteen years ago, giving lie to a statement we've often been guilty of ourselves: "Nothing ever changes in a small town."

By the time we sold the *News,* we had become "oldtimers" in years of service, topped only by Paul Carter, the reluctant proprietor of Hooper's Sooper Appliance Store. Now, three years later, Paul is still in business, and the *News* once again has new owners. Paul is no longer given to drink and is about to be married at the same altar at which he gave his life to the Lord a few weeks ago. The bride-to-be is Polly Wright, the woman who once denounced Paul as hen-pecked. We pray Paul is not another of Polly's "works," but the looks that pass between them say they are in love, and we rejoice for them. The town Polly could not stand has won her heart as surely as Paul has and as surely as God forever changed her—and us.

There have been many changes in three years. Hattie Hooper is dead, another victim of cancer. Patience Sandler has come out of mourning and is dating Silas Monroe. Sonny Sandler, now remarried and a stepfather, continues to operate his father's leather goods store and has expanded into the space formerly occupied by Jim and Ruby Pearl. The Pearls, still alienated from the community because of their business failure, and the Singletons stop by for tea and coffee occasionally. Marty will soon complete college and Russ is back on the road, but they both seem happier than they did when they operated their own Ma-Pa business.

Tom, Dick, the Parson, Peg, Paula, Susan, Cindy, Sarah, Beulah, Pete, Nettie, and Cora still stop in to reminisce. We haven't heard from Bob for years. We don't know if he is still in prison or if he is finally succeeding at life on the outside. We pray it is the latter, but we still cringe at our failure with him. We know now that all do-it-yourself Christianity is destined to fail, but we learned *that* the hard way, much as we learned discipline, duty, and newspapering.

Doug, our once hyperkinetic charmer who hated Ouija, is now a high school junior and on the honor roll. Todd recently returned to college, where he is pursuing a degree in agricultural finance. Both "boys" are over six feet tall, towering over their father and me as they tease us about the silver that crowds the hair that no longer matches the red and brown packets we once found on our living room floor.

Other ghosts, too, have died. Students with learning problems now receive the attention they deserve. The area one-two question has been solved for so long it, too, seems not to have existed.

Time has a way of healing many wounds, of being as fleeting as a will-o' the-wisp. It's hard to believe three years have passed since I wrote that final column.

Three years. "By the end of the third year you should start to show a profit," Marty said long ago. We watched the real estate business she and Russ operated follow the three-year pattern, spiral into six and then nine before they sold it. We watched our own business follow three-year patterns, often reverting to the first of the three with the purchase of new equipment.

Three years. It's too soon to say what will happen by the end of the second three years without the *News,* but it's not too soon to reflect on the past three years, on the five three-year spans that preceded them, and to rejoice at a merciful Father who saw us through them.

Three years. How quickly they pass. Six three-year spans.

Eighteen years. Our hearts have ached, we have been sick and tired, we have felt our stomachs knot with anger and fear, and we know there will be other bruises in the years ahead. But now we know with certainty that our Redeemer lives, that He demands our obedience and our trust. We know He has plans for us as surely as Jeremiah knew when he wrote: "For I know the plans I have for you, says the Lord, plans for welfare and not for evil, to give you a future and a hope."

I know, too, that I will never ride with a camel caravan, that investigative reporting is not my calling, but these fantasies no longer matter. A camel called, but God answered with plans much better than mine.

This book is not one of complaint. It is the true story of an answered prayer written by one of God's slow learners, a popcorn popper become cheerleader for the Lord. It is shared that you, too, may come to know God has plans for each of us, that they unfold, not always on Thursday, but every day of the week.

CHRISTIAN HERALD ASSOCIATION AND ITS MINISTRIES

CHRISTIAN HERALD ASSOCIATION, founded in 1878, publishes The Christian Herald Magazine, one of the leading interdenominational religious monthlies in America. Through its wide circulation, it brings inspiring articles and the latest news of religious developments to many families. From the magazine's pages came the initiative for CHRISTIAN HERALD CHILDREN'S HOME and THE BOWERY MISSION, two individually supported not-for-profit corporations.

CHRISTIAN HERALD CHILDREN'S HOME, established in 1894, is the name for a unique and dynamic ministry to disadvantaged children, offering hope and opportunities which would not otherwise be available for reasons of poverty and neglect. The goal is to develop each child's potential and to demonstrate Christian compassion and understanding to children in need.

Mont Lawn is a permanent camp located in Bushkill, Pennsylvania. It is the focal point of a ministry which provides a healthful "vacation with a purpose" to children who without it would be confined to the streets of the city. Up to 1000 children between the ages of 7 and 11 come to Mont Lawn each year.

Christian Herald Children's Home maintains year-round contact with children by means of an *In-City Youth Ministry*. Central to its philosophy is the belief that only through sustained relationships and demonstrated concern can individual lives be truly enriched. Special emphasis is on individual guidance, spiritual and family counseling and tutoring. This follow-up ministry to inner-city children culminates for many in financial assistance toward higher education and career counseling.

THE BOWERY MISSION, located at 227 Bowery, New York City, has since 1879 been reaching out to the lost men on the Bowery, offering them what could be their last chance to rebuild their lives. Every man is fed, clothed and ministered to. Countless numbers have entered the 90-day residential rehabilitation program at the Bowery Mission. A concentrated ministry of counseling, medical care, nutrition therapy, Bible study and Gospel services awakens a man to spiritual renewal within himself.

These ministries are supported solely by the voluntary contributions of individuals and by legacies and bequests. Contributions are tax deductible. Checks should be made out either to CHRISTIAN HERALD CHILDREN'S HOME or to THE BOWERY MISSION.

Administrative Office: 40 Overlook Drive, Chappaqua, New York 10514
Telephone: (914) 769-9000